The Eternally
Successful
Organization

Other McGraw-Hill Titles by Philip B. Crosby

The Art of Getting Your Own Sweet Way   (1972, 1981)
Quality Is Free: The Art of Making Quality Certain   (1979)
Quality Without Tears: The Art of Hassle-Free Management   (1984)
Running Things: The Art of Making Things Happen   (1986)

The Eternally Successful Organization

The Art of Corporate Wellness

Philip B. Crosby

McGraw-Hill Book Company

New York   St. Louis   San Francisco   Auckland
Bogotá   Hamburg   London   Madrid   Mexico
Milan   Montreal   New Delhi   Panama
Paris   São Paulo   Singapore
Sydney   Tokyo   Toronto

Library of Congress Cataloging-in-Publication Data

Crosby, Philip B.
  The eternally successful organization.

  Includes index.
  1. Organizational behavior. 2. Management.
I. Title.
HD58.7.C75 1988   658.4   87-37853
ISBN 0-07-014533-4

1234567890 DOC/DOC 89210987

ISBN 0-07-014533-4

*The editors for this book were William Sabin, James Bessent, and
Barbara B. Toniolo, the designer was Naomi Auerbach, and the
production supervisor was Suzanne Babeuf. It was composed by the
McGraw-Hill Book Company Professional & Reference Division
Composition Unit.*

Printed and bound by R. R. Donnelley & Sons Company.

NOTE: *A sixty-minute audio program to accompany this book
is now available. Ask for it at your local bookstore or phone
toll-free 1-800-2-MCGRAW.*

Dedicated to the memory of my parents

Contents

Part 3. The Quest Continues

Preface

This book has been cooking in my mind for years. It is my "time-is-probably-running-out" contribution to try once more to help save American management from itself. For 35 years I have been showing and preaching the benefits of running operations differently from traditional practice. I have been recounting the advantages of preventing rather than fixing. Unfortunately no one is against preventing; it's just that they don't have time right now.

Outside of hanging around with a sign that said: "Repent, the end is near," my planned approach has been as always low-key and fairly subtle. I have always tried to help individuals discover it all for themselves, not beat it into their bones. But now I am overmature and not quite so patient. In 10 years I may have resigned myself to what appears to be inevitable. So I am going at it a little more directly.

When Philip Crosby Associates (PCA) was formed in 1979, I had no notion that it would become a large complex organization operating worldwide. Luckily the only organizational approach I knew was a formal one, learned in 28 years with large public companies. So we began that way even when there were only two or three of us.

Through these years I have come to realize that there is a lot involved in running a company that has little to do with the content of the management systems. It all has to do with people: If we take care of the customers and the employees, everything else takes care of itself. It is hard to find an organization that both customers and employees regard with continuous affection and appreciation.

PCA has been a marvelous experience. The marketing strategy has been that clients would have to come to the conclusion that they needed to improve quality, and then find us. We would help the media write about us, but we would not advertise or solicit. We don't even make sales calls.

The reason for this is that executives cannot be sold into being serious about quality; they have to make the decision themselves, and in their own time. What we would do is establish a credibility through the work we did and wait for calls to come in. I liken it to running a heart transplant clinic. It would be difficult to entice someone to come and get a new heart without conclusive proof that it is necessary. Like improving quality, that is something it is hard to talk a person into doing. But we wanted them to know we were there when the time came.

PCA has grown into a truly international company with education and implementation taught and conducted in a dozen languages. It has a fully funded pension plan and has birthed several wealthy and dozens of well-off people through stock options and gifts. The clients have all benefited from the company's work, as PCA has benefited from their support. All this came about with no government help or hindrance. It is a clear case of what can happen in a free market. I wish that all nations could trust their citizens enough to let them take such a succeed-or-fail route.

Now this book is not a description of how PCA is run or what a wonderful job we did in making it all happen. We had a lot of problems—from embezzlement to zero cash flow—

and the company has not quite lived "eternally," not yet anyway. But it served as a personal laboratory and foundation that I could use in observing things at close hand while dealing with clients in dozens of different businesses all over the world. There is no substitute for combat when it comes to learning the difference between keeping your head down and raising it.

My previous book, *Running Things*, represented a departure from my usual writing on quality management. It did include some material on the overall importance of quality in making things happen as planned. In every operation one thought process follows another. I like to think of *Quality Is Free, Quality Without Tears, Running Things*, and *The Eternally Successful Organization* as four books that cover the broad field of management. Actually they relate to the Maturity Grid in *Quality Is Free.*

My first-ever book, *Cutting the Cost of Quality*, is way out of print and unlamented. It related to Uncertainty, the first step of the grid; *Quality Is Free* related to Awareness; *Quality Without Tears* to Enlightment; *Running Things* to Wisdom; and this book to Certainty. *The Art of Getting Your Own Sweet Way* applies all along the way to personal management.

Since I am unlikely to write a book on accounting or investing, there is no plan to produce an entire do-it-yourself library. No one knows enough useful things to do that.

But as I learn how to do something, usually the hard way, I like to share my new-found knowledge with the thought that it might make things easier for others. The advice that people need in order to make their lives less stressful and more useful is usually not a big item.

I can remember when $500 would have turned my life around. If someone had taken enough interest to show me how to get out of that mess, I would have avoided a great deal of pain. I think of that and other situations every time I pay the check in a New York restaurant.

We go to Georgia, to the Landings in Savannah, each month for a week or so in order to rest and write. It is impossible to write in my office, and I find it difficult to keep my former habit of writing late at night or early in the morning in my den at home.

I would like to thank my assistant, Debbie Eifert, for her help in pulling the text together. The experience of dealing with floppy disks rather than paper is still something strange to me. I have to secretly print it out now and then to feel as if something is there.

I have appreciated the counsel and support provided by PCA client executives. From the supersized companies to ones smaller than PCA, they have openly shared their concerns and advice with me. There is a lot of useful knowledge out there; getting it in a form so that others will use it is the challenge.

Thank you.

PHILIP B. CROSBY
Winter Park, Florida

PART 1

A Prescription for Corporate Health

1
Introduction— Why Not?

In order to place this book in its proper perspective, it might be helpful to examine some of the thought sequences that brought it about. It has been a long time developing. I liked the creative process much better the way they did it in the old MGM movies. The hero had a blinding flash of inspiration, and the next thing we knew the book was written, music and lyrics materialized, and everyone was dancing and singing about it. But then, not everything is as it seems.

I remember Ernie Kovacs, the comedian, used to tell a story about a little Princess who took a frog home and put it under her pillow, and the next morning, when she awoke, there beside her in the bed was a handsome young Prince.

"And to this very day," Kovacs would leer, "that girl's mother does not believe this story."

About four years after I started to work for real, it began to dawn on me that I knew almost nothing about the business that employed me. Oh I knew how to do my job, which was being a reliability engineer, and I was coming to grips with my own concepts of quality management, but I didn't know how the business worked. In college I had concentrated on medical subjects, so what I knew about business was learned in business. My world began at the front door of the shop and ended on the shipping dock. Also, I had no comprehension of why one company was successful and one wasn't. I wasn't clear on what success was for that matter. Everyone just sort of knew who was successful. The primary measurement characteristic was how much money the company made; the second was how long it had been around.

I was beginning to wonder about things. It was a similar experience to awakening at age six to the thought that there were a lot of chimneys in the world and how could one large man get down all of them in one night. Until this time I had always assumed that everyone else knew a lot more about everything than I did. I had placed myself in the role of a natural born follower, as they say in my home state of West Virginia.

The companies I first worked with concentrated primarily on defense products, specifically the missile business, and their world centered around the Department of Defense (DOD). Why we won or lost contracts was a complete mystery to me. We would make proposals to the DOD, it would obtain similar ones from other potential suppliers, and someone would get the contract. I never knew why specific awards went to one company or the other but always assumed that the better proposal was the winner. The main concern at my level was whether there might be some promotions or overtime available if new contracts came through.

In looking back at that time I realize that my coworkers would have been pleased to share information with me. I just didn't know enough about it all even to ask questions. That happened to me recently when I was at a golf charity event and stood for a few moments chatting with Arnold Palmer and Greg Norman, who are, of course, world famous professional competitors in the game. As a lifetime golfer of a completely different caliber, I couldn't even think of anything interesting to ask them. They were obviously used to such a situation, so we talked about business and they asked me questions about quality. That is one subject everyone feels comfortable discussing since we are all customers and entitled to not be disappointed.

My experience in school had been that I occasionally had a different view from the conventional and accepted one. This was not for the purpose of being troublesome but just because I wanted things to make sense to me. Once in a while what was being taught just didn't quite fit together for me, but my data bank was not large enough for me to know whether I was correct or not. Teachers had large data banks and seemed very positive about what they knew.

As a result I became convinced, by the treatment of my teachers and fellow students, that I was not as bright as everyone else. I still think that way, but now it is a useful position because I can look at things with an open mind since I am not expected to know all about whatever comes up. What I began to understand in business was that the criterion for being a successful person was the ability to get something done—a simple truth, but one that eluded me for years. If one could produce, and was a halfway reasonable person, there was an open road ahead. Once I began to read business magazines and to apply some of the thoughts that appeared in my own mind, it all became much less complex. I found that managers really wanted some help and that they appreciated what I did. It was a whole new lease on life.

I remember my first exposure to an assembly operation in a missile plant. I had moved there as a reliability engineer and was assigned to assembly with the job of preventing problems. While trying to figure out what went where and why, I began to plot the assembly line in a flowchart format. Everything that someone was mounting had to come from somewhere and be fastened to something that came from somewhere else.

I spent about two weeks on the chart doing that in between chasing problems. I got all involved with laying it out on a long sheet of paper using different shaped blocks for different missile and supply systems. It was a lot of fun. When the chart was about complete, I had one aspect that I couldn't figure out, so I took it to my boss and asked for guidance.

"Where did you get this?" he asked. He was astounded that such a piece of paper existed. Everyone wanted copies and I was an instant hero. (A little later my chart was classified "Top Secret" which was one level above my clearance—so I never saw it again.) That is when I began to realize that hardly anyone knew anything about what was happening except in his or her own area of work. From then on I made it my business to try to understand the work of others and offer to help them. They were usually grateful enough to teach me what they knew about it. It doesn't take long in any organization before one can have a broader view of what is happening than most other folks.

My first real exposure to management at the actual decision level started when I began attending Harold Geneen's monthly general management meeting (GMM) on the 40th floor of the ITT Americas Building in New York. I was a corporate vice president, responsible for quality worldwide, and stayed at International Telephone & Telegraph (IT&T) for 14 fascinating years. The GMM was a wide-open meeting where everything was up for discussion. I soon learned that I could understand things as well as anyone else and that no one was expected to know everything. It was all right not to know—at least the first time—and one could dig into a subject until it was clear. This was a great breakthrough for me personally.

Each month at the GMM the senior executives of the corporation gathered for three days of examining what was going on. No sparrow fell anywhere in the world of IT&T that its autopsy was not reviewed in detail. This was useful to me because everything we did was based one way or another on this information exchange. The week following the general management meeting many of the same people went to Brussels for a week of pouring over the status of the European operations. Many fallen sparrows had the honor of being discussed two weeks in a row.

The GMM would begin with the comptroller displaying everyone's numbers on the screens in the room. Each group, then division, then unit, was up there to see. Negative numbers had brackets around them. Inventory, accounts receivable, quality, every imaginable figure was displayed. It took forever and was not always interesting, but it had to be done that way to show that there was no place to hide anything.

Then the groups would talk one at a time. Each executive would discuss the current status, specifically any changes that might have occurred since his or her letter was written. I forgot to mention that each executive, from plant manager up, wrote a monthly letter to Geneen concerning the status of the operation. This was accomplished according to a predetermined format. The results were placed in two 3-ring notebooks that each of us received a few days before the meeting. Unfortunately for us, Geneen actually read them all and made notes. Thus he knew what was supposed to be happening (he remembered that from the business plan meetings), and he knew what people said was happening. Discussing those differences—that was what took the three days.

He always approached each discussion with an open, and well informed, mind. The executive would talk about what was happening and what the future looked like. At the completion of this 10-minute or so informal presentation, Geneen or another member of the office of the chairman would ask questions, searching for weak spots that they had perhaps been worrying about. Individual staff people would then bring up any subject that concerned them. I usually discussed my items with any potential offenders during breaks. It was very easy to get their attention when the alternative was open disclosure.

The meeting was conducted frankly and openly for the most part; it was all positive. The assumption was that everyone was trying to do the right thing. However, the slightest sign of uncertainty or "weaselwording" was enough to bring forth intense questioning. These incidents were the cause of the fearful reputation the meeting earned over the years. The boss took all this very seriously and expected others to do the same. There was a large corporate staff to help, although not all members thought helping was their main purpose.

"Getting the story out so the company could do well" was the theme of all these sessions, and for the most part they were useful and productive; I learned a lot. During these IT&T years I was exposed to about every kind of business situation that can occur. I once offered to pay for my education, but Geneen said the accounting department would not be able to figure what to do with the money.

People always ask me about Geneen's "system" of management. Actually he didn't have a system; he just wanted to know everything about everything that was going on. Accomplishing that required a lot of data generation, meetings, and staff support. He didn't arrange all that for our benefit; he did it for himself. And I must say that it worked well, he seemed to know everything. That is the only place I have ever been where the management at all levels was so well informed. But it could wear you out. I became adept at not going to planned meetings so I could get out in the real world and help make quality happen.

When I started my own company, I realized that I knew much more than the average "starter-upper," but not nearly as much as I thought I did. Knowing how to handle an international managerial problem was of little help when it came to figuring out leases in Central Florida. But with my newfound confidence I just plowed right ahead. The key element was making my own decisions after getting opinions from professionals such as accountants, lawyers, and people in other small businesses.

As a management consultant I have had the privilege of working closely with a large number of corporations of all sizes. I have spent time with their employees, customers, and suppliers. I know many chief executive officers (CEOs) very well. I spend a lot of time "keeping up" with what is going on in the world.

As an author I find that people talk with me about whatever interests them. They feel as if they know me. People walk up and begin a conversation as if we had been college roommates. The act of laying out money to buy a book full of opinions and experience seems to also purchase a relationship that doesn't exist in other professional situations.

It is a completely different environment from that in which people approach me as a quality "guru." At that time they usually want to discuss some philosophical point or encourage me to beat up on some industry or company. They think I can get the offenders to straighten out by threatening to break their legs. I find the guru business tiresome. The business media assign that name to anyone who has a following in any field. I wish they would be a little more original. Quality is a serious matter and should be treated that way.

My mind is tuned to gathering bits and pieces of information that eventually glump together into some sort of awareness. My favorite reading matter is biographical and historical. In addition to those really interesting sources, I also read through magazines devoted to business, travel, social commentary, and other topics. I even read *The Enquirer.*

This daily habit has completely reversed my feelings of 34 years ago when I thought everyone else understood everything. Now I realize, just as they do, that we all comprehend only a small portion of the complete picture. Even Geneen's "system" produced only a small understanding of what those 400,000 people in 60 countries were doing with the assets and customers of the company. It may not be possible to know what is happening in any significant detail. Each company's GMM may be equivalent to only a gossip session.

Yet there have been very successful corporations, volunteer organizations, nations, governments, cities, explorations, foundations, farms, businesses, and other human endeavors. Many books have been written about them, their methods have been studied, and all of us have admired their accomplishments. As far as we know, they did not necessarily have a marvelous internal data or status system in common, but they were successful.

So how come a successful organization does not maintain that level of accomplishment continuously? Why does it seem that there must be an inevitable backsliding, turnaround, and redoing? What would business magazines write about if organizations could indeed present constant achievement?

We see many cases where the apparently invincible organization becomes vulnerable seemingly overnight. The giants of this generation have all had to run hard to catch up: Chrysler, Lockheed, IBM, General Motors, Xerox, General Electric, among others. They had the assets and people to recover but may never be the same. GM spent $40 billion trying to change and still lost market share. It is turning around, but slowly.

The world changes continually, and often executives are too busy pattering along their well-worn road to notice it. There certainly was adequate warning about foreign competition in automobiles, copiers, televisions, computers, and other products. Yet industries ignored this threat and concentrated on competing against their fellow domestic corporations. The entire Japanese automobile industry, for instance, could have been purchased, or joined as a partner, for peanuts in the early 1970s. In 1986 Japan produced more vehicles than any other nation. Corporate and industry culture let the companies down in that case. The leaders thought they knew all there was to know about the business now and forever. Being convinced that one knows the whole picture is the surest way to failure, as we all know.

Someone or some group or some system has to actually run things. Often the successful organization revolves around a single person with an intuitive sense of what has to be done and who can do it. This person may or may not be the titular head of the operation but is clearly the thought leader and the engine that drives everything. When that person is gone or becomes ineffective, there can be a dramatic alteration in the way everything occurs.

Usually, though, the cause is not that clear. Things just seem to begin to rust out, or perhaps the deterioration due to time is noticed when there is no one to make adjustments. The planning system that worked so well doesn't work any more; customers who were unswervingly loyal are committing economic adultery; the apolitical environment in the company has collapsed; and nest building is going on everywhere. Communication has ceased, employees are grumbling, and the sharks begin to get interested.

It is a rare case when a culture exists that will let an organization survive such an experience without dramatic change. The butterfly has become a sloth. Instead of soaring about the sky, drinking from beckoning flowers, and being admired by all, the organization suddenly is dull, gray, plodding, and not very interesting. Effectiveness is not a consideration. Same people, same markets, same products, different policies.

I probably will not be here for eternity, so I will never know if the thoughts in the following pages will work all that long. I do know that they would have prevented many of the managerial problems I have observed in the last 30 years. This is because most organizations have what appear to me to be suicidal tendencies. They do themselves in rather than being bumped off by others.

When everything is moving along well, they just sort of doze off—or something. Suddenly one day the salespeople are spending 75 percent of their time planning and doing administrative tasks, leaving 25 percent for the customer. Debt begins to rise; accounts receivable age faster; bright young people begin to drift off to other companies; a huge new headquarters building gets built; customers are becoming neglected; housekeeping noticeably deteriorates; and management doesn't seem to notice.

It takes a lot of cooperative foolishness to reach this point. Eventually someone will notice what is happening, or read about it in *Forbes,* or get a letter from a corporate raider, or come to work someday to find the place is gone. Wouldn't it be nice if managers knew what to concentrate on in order to be consistently successful? They would have to learn to avoid fads and to believe the measurements, of course. Most problems are avoidable but are rarely seen by those involved. The victim is always the last to know.

Organizations don't start out to be losers; they have the right principles, the proper ideas—they just lose the pitch and forget the tune somewhere along the line. Cities that begin to lose business, people, culture, and such are usually surprised to learn that they are considered to be difficult to deal with. You have to be a superdedicated person to open a store in New York City, for instance. Dealing with the various government agencies and getting material in and out of the city itself is the masterpiece of challenges.

Companies find their customers and employees turning away from them. The new headquarters building that was planned as a symbol of power and competence becomes an embarrassing white elephant. For no good (or at least apparent) reason, management peers in the industry begin to find fault with the company's performance, and Wall Street starts to worry. The organization is turning brown around the edges, and there seems to be little reason for it. The Board often becomes difficult about capital investment and uses the assets to keep on paying dividends. Several middle management staffers, whose potential is unappreciated, leave causing no stir at all. No one even knew they could be valuable.

In social or cultural organizations this pattern reveals itself in different ways: support begins to waver; new Board members find reasons to leave; customers or clients begin to complain about lack of attention or compassion; participation declines; the local newspaper begins to make a negative comment now and then.

People can't last forever; the body eventually wears out. There is no way to prevent that from happening. But organizations have no need to die. They can continually be reformed and shaped to meet and overcome the age of that moment. They can be continuously useful rather than add to the turbulence that we make of the world. They can provide something dependable rather than yet another source of disappointment.

We don't need to go through the business of having thousands of people out of work because their industry has become economically extinct, such as we see around the coal and steel areas. Suddenly the individual workers and the company itself do not know what to do. They have been led to believe that life would continue exactly as it had been for the past several generations. They felt no need to learn something else; they were misled and personally negligent. But the pain is real, and it doesn't have to happen like that. Growing and maturing provide their own pain, but it should be a pleasant sensation, worth the effort.

Companies and people tend to fail eventually when they become locked into one format or culture. That locking can occur from something no more complicated than naming the company. The Universal Buggy Whip Corporation could get to thinking it is in the buggy whip business.

When the employees and suppliers of an organization do things correctly on a routine basis; when customers are pleased that their needs are anticipated and met; when growth is internally generated, profitable, and planned; when change is welcomed and implemented to advantage; and when everyone enjoys working there—the foundation of an eternally successful organization exists.

Why shouldn't it be that way? After all, management is charged with making the venture successful and compensated with that in mind. No charters are issued with permission to be unsuccessful; society does not admire failure. Yet it will be said that becoming eternally successful is unattainable in the world of reality. It will be put forth that such a consistency is not in tune with the abilities of those who manage companies or other organizations.

However, it is within their capability if they are oriented in the proper direction, have the proper information, and choose to do so. The personal agenda that individuals select lies within themselves but can be influenced dramatically by the goals of the organization and the obligations of the individuals to it. The most consistently successful of all enterprises seem to be those that are "family" managed (the extended family, which includes all the employees, not just people with the same name). The executives have a commitment that is larger than that to the business; it is to the other members of the family, both present and future.

Every decision is based on, "What is good for the family?"

As a result, it becomes possible to move out of declining areas of activity into those with more potential. The family is more important than the product or service of that company. The company does not become entombed in one field of endeavor. Many of these organizations wind up in finance in one way or another.

Professional executives are more likely to be loyal to the company and its products than to the stockholders. Usually they do not own much stock personally. The typical proxy statement shows that the outside directors typically only have a token amount of shares. I like it better when their personal survival depends on the vitality of the company. I cannot recall a single meeting conversation about doing anything for the stockholders in all my years of working for large companies. The talk is always about the market, finance, and products. It is assumed that we will have the stockholder in mind at all times, so people never mention it except when they want to win an argument by getting sympathy for someone.

However, if a product line, or the corporation itself, begins to fall on hard times, the executives know they can move on to another company and will not even be missed after a few months. They don't always have to live with the consequences of their action or lack of it; they can join another wagon train. The shareholders can handle their part of a downside situation by selling out to others, who expect less, and life moves on. It would seem that no one is anchored to the place after all.

The other side of this is the reason colleges and some other nonprofit organizations muddle through over the years. They are not wonderfully managed, but they have abundant loyalty from administrators, faculty, alumni, students, and the community. This creates a glue that assures consistent overcoming.

Over the years traditions are built that are not taken lightly by these institutions. James Hilton's *Goodbye Mr. Chips* tells the tale of one professor who deals with several generations of "boys" at an English public school. The school rises above them all, and even as they go out into the world they never forget where their loyalty lies. Of course they have only spent a small percentage of their days at the old blue. Some companies have achieved this old school tie feeling and used it to advantage. But eventually and inevitably it begins to deteriorate when faced with the untraditional changes that are brought about by an unsympathetic management reacting to what it considers an unfeeling marketplace. Companies can completely reverse themselves in a week. What was important becomes repulsive.

Becoming eternally successful seems to me to combine (1) the concern for long-range success that is found in family organizations with (2) the loyalty-producing characteristics of a small college and driving it all with (3) the efficiency of the professionally managed, and therefore heartless, corporation.

We would need to provide balances in order to overcome the negative side of each type. Family businesses sometimes come apart because of disagreements between family members that have nothing to do with business. Colleges fail to grow or respond because the administrators are intimidated by the faculty or vice versa. And conventional organizations fail for all the conventional reasons we read about in *Fortune, Forbes,* and *Business Week*—mostly executive ego.

So we need to find a way to incorporate the concern found in family, the loyalty found in education, and the skills found in professional management—all in the same management concept. Management needs to have a structured foundation that figures in every action it takes. This needs to be in place consistently if success is to be eternal and the company is to be there forever. Just as the human body has a built-in mechanism to breathe without conscious thought, so the organization can survive only when its immune system is designed to operate automatically.

To make that happen the management policy of the organization needs to be constructed around the following five considerations. All of them require continuous action and monitoring. They are all equal in importance because they feed on each other. A company that is going to be eternally successful will have these easily identifiable characteristics:

- People do things right routinely.
- Growth is profitable and steady.
- Customer needs are anticipated.
- Change is planned and managed.
- People are proud to work there.

Each of these will be examined on its own in a chapter bearing its name and then brought together in a case history. They sound quite basic, and they are. But if they can exist all the time in an organization, it will exist all the time. There is no reason why it should not be so if the management can agree to accomplish it.

These characteristics are readily measurable. Implementing them is well within the competence of any management that can understand a balance sheet and is people-oriented. In fact everyone does something about them anyway; people don't just put it all together as the foundation of the management culture. If they had learned to think this way, American managers may not have been totally surprised and economically overcome by being tossed into a world market. Managers would have anticipated it and been ready to lead the way instead of paddling furiously just to keep from being swept over the falls.

As the company gets easier to manage, pitfalls are avoided because there are no secrets, and the personal success of the manager is assured. They will remember us as affectionately after retirement as they do Mr. Chips. What is there to look forward to now? Who had that job during the last generation? Does anyone remember or care? The business of continuing a company for the future is a challenge that is not only worthy but provides the opportunity for immortality.

2

The Advantage
of Being Eternally
Successful

Every organization has some success at some time, even if
only a great opening night. Unfortunately, the criteria we all
use to measure success relate soley to past performance. The
record revenues and earnings announced in this year's annual report were accomplished in a world that exists no
more. The people who caused it to happen are now a year
older and different. The customers who purchased the
goods and services may have new needs. The organization
may be contracting a case of lockjaw, for all we know.

In business, past is not necessarily prologue.

Organizations must remain living, breathing, alert organ-
isms if they are going to be able to handle what is going to
happen. Nothing can be taken as permanent. A continual,
and formal, preparation of the organization to handle the future, along with reevaluation of resource management, is the
price of avoiding the quicksand.

We all know of housing developments where the sales reps
sell a little more each year and are rewarded for it. As time

goes by, they become more entrenched, handling resales as well as new properties. Then one day the place is finished; there is no room for new homes. This comes as a shock to all involved. Even though they have been planning for this, talking about it, and assuming its inevitability—it is as though they thought it would never actually take place.

They have been going ahead on a personal basis as though the sales commissions for new homes would last forever and grow each year. The "salesperson of the year" suddenly has nothing to sell. The world of resale is not controllable; other brokers enter the market; a new level of competition now exists. The little office with signs directing potential buyers to it is gone. No more balloons, no advertising, no model homes. The world has changed, and they were not prepared for it.

As management teams sit down to create strategies designed to get them through the coming years, they have a hard time looking forward. Organizations don't begin with a clean sheet of paper each year. There is no building with completely empty offices or empty warehouses. A lot of things have been put in motion and cannot be turned around that easily. Also there are areas of privilege that have ways of not being tampered with.

People and systems get entrenched, so much that they exist only for themselves. If a company has at least two departments in its headquarters, it doesn't need any field operations for them to monitor. Staffers of the two departments can have full careers just working on each other. People can stay in the same activity too long. Wouldn't it be wonderful if everyone could change jobs every couple of years? The comptroller who is always complaining about the expense accounts of Marketing and Sales could run those departments. At least we wouldn't have to listen to the same stories every meeting.

The eternally successful organization (ESO) does not have to contend with uneven times and is assured that survival is only an academic question. Every year it is up another large percentage in everything, and the only question is whether it will rise or fall on the "Most Admired Company" list—life on a stable platform, so to speak.

All this requires a lot of work and the ability to prepare for what is yet to come. But if we look at industries and companies that have suddenly found themselves floundering, it is easy to see through our rearview mirror that the writing was on the wall all along.

In the ESO, wall reading is a requirement. This is not a matter of deciphering Turkish tea remains, or examining chicken entrails, or trying to find two economists who agree. The wall I am talking about is where the business is displayed every day: the marketplace.

The information is there, and it is recognized by customers, by employees, by the media. They may not know how to describe it exactly, but it is there. It may also be delivered directly. President Franklin Roosevelt was visited by Albert Einstein, who told him that it was possible to build an atomic weapon and that the Germans were working on it. Roosevelt listened. The U.S. automobile industry was warned that there would be an oil shortage; it was warned that it had better do something about quality. The leaders refused to listen.

I personally spent years to no avail trying to get someone interested in quality. And I was, like the oil economists, doing it for free.

Every business changes every day in some way. The successful ones learn how to recognize and even create these changes. Most organizations do not do this. A quick review of what has happened in the past few years might emphasize this.

Oil. In 1974, when oil was $3 a barrel, everyone was making money. Now that it is several times that amount, the U.S. contingent anyway is broke and struggling. This came about through unrealistic borrowing and spending. There is no oil fairy. The world's largest industry is still oil.

Steel. "It costs so much to ship steel from Japan to the United States that we never have to worry about it." That is what steel executives used to say back in the early 1970s. They used cash flow to pay dividends instead of updating their processes, while insisting on carrying full lines of products whether they made money or not.

Autos. These companies used to make a lot of money in a market of 6 million vehicles a year. Now, because of overhead (much of which came from "give-them-what-they-want-but-keep-the-lines-moving" labor settlements), lack of interest in quality, and managerial arrogance, they have had to turn themselves inside out to be where they used to be. Half the market went to others in the process. Now they are coming back and doing well. But nothing will ever be the same.

Television Sets. Having dedicated itself to running a wonderful home service repair system ("the works in a drawer"), this industry fought for tariff protection instead of learning how to made sets that were reliable.

Semiconductors. They concentrated on "economic yields" rather than learning how to make the product, and they indulged in price wars at the same time. As a result the gains made by research were wasted by "commodity" thinking.

Franchising. Lack of training for the managers, tricky financial maneuvering, and variable product integrity turned this into a risky business.

Airlines. Working on the basis that their customers were more interested in ticket price than in arriving on time, or being served properly, the airlines have launched a continuous price war. Airlines are run by people who have never flown like normal folks. They were pilots or well cared for executives. Airports are designed by those who never travel, apparently.

Health Care. Physicians wouldn't let anyone run the health care industry, so costs went out of sight, and now the insurance companies and health maintenance organizations

(HMOs) are taking over. Thus, practicing medicine is no fun anymore; it's like being in Britain. Soon patients will be assigned, except for the very rich. Hospitals are being bought up and run "efficiently" through mass purchasing and fewer laboratory tests.

Banks.   In the race to grow, banks let themselves into making large loans to anyone who didn't mind premium interest rates. Therefore, buildings were built only because money was available, and foreign nations learned to live well without producing anything salable. But banks were very difficult on local small businesses in order to keep the loan default ratio down so the loan officers would look good. Now banks are giving people lines of credit on the equity in their homes. This means that some people will soon lose their primary source of personal wealth, that equity. When it comes time to sell, they will not be able to buy another home. We will become a nation of renters and landlords.

Churches.   The traditional Protestant churches ignored the Charismatic Movement by not understanding that people just wanted a little joy in their worship. As a result millions are switching denominations. The Catholic Church refuses to pay any attention to its members and conducts a monologue, thinking that someone is listening. People are too busy wondering to do much worshiping. Jews have gone from one standard congregation to many, with the variation being how "reformed" they are. Middle-eastern Moslems are so busy insisting on having it all one way that they are causing their nations to regress.

Discounters.   After making life miserable for traditional retailers, the discounters turned traditional and began offering services that the others did. As a result, no one is doing well since none of them remember how to do service properly. People aren't trained, well paid, or placed about in sufficient numbers. It needs to begin all over again.

Commercial Real Estate. Every town seems to have too much commercial property. See "Banks."

The above few troubled industries are only briefly mentioned. In every one what was going to happen was known by many but not accepted by those in control. If these industries had been concerned about getting things done right the first time, growing through what they knew, managing change, developing new products, and having happy employees—they might not have taken their eyes off the important things. In that proper kind of environment, with a proper navigational heading, everyone benefits continually. Customers, employees, stockholders, management will have fulfilled and serving lives. Challenges will be there continually, but they will be recognized and dealt with to advantage. Management won't have to be so defensive that nothing moves without its personal touch.

The Eternally Successful Organization Grid, which follows, is intended to provide an overview of the progress that can be made with a thoughtful and deliberate approach.

It is useful if you find your place on the grid before starting the next chapter. No one need know.

	COMATOSE	INTENSIVE CARE	PROGRESSIVE CARE	HEALING	WELLNESS
QUALITY	Nobody does anything right around here. *Price of Nonconformance = 33%*	We finally have a list of customer complaints. *Price of Nonconformance = 28%*	We are beginning a formal Quality Improvement Process. *Price of Nonconformance = 20%*	Customer complaints are practically gone. *Price of Nonconformance = 13%*	People do things right the first time routinely. *Price of Nonconformance = 3%*
GROWTH	Nothing ever changes. *Return after tax = nil*	We bought a turkey. *Return after tax = nil*	The new product isn't too bad. *Return after tax = 3%*	The new group is growing well. *Return after tax = 7%*	Growth is profitable and steady. *Return after tax = 12%*
CUSTOMERS	Nobody ever orders twice. *Customer complaints on orders = 63%*	Customers don't know what they want. *Customer complaints on orders = 54%*	We are working with customers. *Customer complaints on orders = 26%*	We are making many defect-free deliveries. *Customer complaints on orders = 9%*	Customer needs are anticipated. *Customer complaints on orders = 0%*
CHANGE	Nothing ever changes. *Changes controlled by Systems Integrity = 0%*	Nobody tells anyone anything. *Changes controlled by Systems Integrity = 2%*	We need to know what is happening. *Changes controlled by Systems Integrity = 55%*	There is no reason for anyone to be surprised. *Changes controlled by Systems Integrity = 85%*	Change is planned and managed. *Changes controlled by Systems Integrity = 100%*
EMPLOYEES	This place is a little better than not working. *Employee turnover = 65%*	Human Resources has been told to help employees. *Empoyee turnover = 45%*	Error Cause Removal programs have been started. *Employee turnover = 40%*	Career path evaluations are implemented now. *Employee turnover = 7%*	People are proud to work here. *Employee turnover = 2%*

3

People Do Things Right Routinely

If we trace the history of management from the beginning of recorded history through the latest copy of *The New York Times* Sunday edition, we find very little thought given to the possibility that people could ever be counted on to do things right routinely. Much more attention has been bestowed on developing effective corrective action programs or "idiot-proof" processes. When it has been essential that exact obedience be required, at least for a short time period, the craft of intimidation was refined. Basic training in every trade counts on browbeating to get the novice's attention.

Over the years intimidation slowly evolved into the more positive art of motivation. Men like Charles Schwab, Henry Ford I (he really was a genius at it—early on), and Napoleon showed that people could be led so they would rise to their potential. But there is no evidence that being willing to die for a cause, or a monthly output, produces any more consistent dedication to error-free operation than being left unmotivated. In fact, many of the worst situations are caused by those whose devotion overrode the laws of the land or the prudence of their position. Watergate would fit into that description, or insider trading, or Iranscam. In all those cases the primary motive of the individual was not personal financial gain. They did what they did in order to prove that they, or their cause, was right—or perhaps just to show that they were superior to the rest of the world. I'm sure they never took seriously the thought that it might have been illegal.

We have all seen situations in which a group of people were brought together in an environment where it was important that things be done correctly, and it actually came about. It may have been nothing more significant than a school play, but it did indeed occur. If such things do not regularly occur, the failure is in lack of leadership and example. It is not because of human frailty.

One well-known group that learned to do things right the first time was the Green Bay Packers under Coach Vince Lombardi. The team members were excellent athletes, but not beyond what was to be found on other league football teams. The plays designed by the coaching staff were rather routine; they didn't invent a new, mysterious formation that guaranteed victory. Yet for a few years they were the best in every department. They learned to perform the basics without error. They would block, tackle, run, and otherwise perform their assigned tasks with confidence and reliability. They could depend on each other. A strong discipline, built on respect, held them together and helped them pay attention to the job at hand.

The same situation happens in business organizations, but team sports, particularly football, lend themselves to a quicker understanding of this phenomenon. The outstanding teams are invariably said to have accomplished their victories by "execution." Fortunately, this is not the same context as the fictional Banana Republic system of achievement. Here execution means that each person performed his assigned task completely, at the correct time. It also means that each of those tasks was just exactly what needed to be done at each of those moments.

Within the last two sentences we have the entire world of management obligation. Management is supposed to cause

- Each person
- To perform his or her assigned task
- Completely
- At the correct time
- Each of these tasks to be just exactly what needed to be done at the proper moment

How can this be made to happen, happen, and happen— routinely? Is that within the capacity of normal people? After all, very few of the great leaders ever get through their career without failing, sometimes dramatically. Is there some inevitability within the process itself that says that what goes up must come down?

There is no reason I know of that it should be out of reach. Those who go up do so by their own efforts, and they usually come down because they forgot what it was that took them up. Many times they begin to believe their own success stories. They get away from the basic execution that caused it all in the first place. And causing it all in the first place is a matter of understanding what is involved and wanting to do that. Most people have good intentions but don't produce the results they dream about. They don't take time to really understand what is behind the veils shielding complete comprehension. And behind the next layer too.

Each Person.   "Each person," for instance, involves a lot of people. We are not talking just about those who are in a football uniform, or working in a plant, or at a certain level of management. In fact, the players themselves often are not the primary ingredient of a successful team. Some who are breathtakingly outstanding with one group can't hold on to the ball when they join another. I have known many executives who were promoted from a job they had mastered into one completely incomprehensible to them.

One never knows what one can do. I remember that as a 17-year-old senior I was barely able to make the track squad and, in fact, did so only as a member of the mile relay team. My position on that squad, third, was traditionally served by the slowest member. This fit in accurately with the rest of my running career over the four years in high school.

However, a month after track season ended I entered the Navy and was sent off to boot camp. Within a few weeks I found myself running track at speeds I didn't know I was capable of and actually setting a record for completing the obstacle course. The chief had selected me from the crowd based on his guess of my athletic ability. He told the others that I would show them how to do the obstacle course and assured me that I would be great, and I was off. No one ever came near the time I established including, on other occasions, myself. As I look back, I realize that it was the first time in my life that anyone ever seemed to think that I could do something well that required large amounts of perspiration. Fortunately all that has worn off, and I have essentially retired from athletic competition.

But I have never forgotten the effect that coaching and confidence could have on one person. It made me realize that very few people ever reach their potential because they don't know what it is and no one helps them. We can spend our whole lives underachieving.

In an organization, the description "each person" does not automatically apply just to the "line" people, those who touch what goes out of the place. In fact, it has to include those who affect the operation and may not be a direct part of it, such as suppliers, advisors, or even family. There has to be a complete environment of involvement, and the leadership has to cause that to happen.

To Perform His or Her Assigned Task.   The only job I ever had where my boss explained it all clearly to me was when I drove a trash truck at Oglebay Park in Wheeling, West Virginia, one summer. Each picnic site had at least one 55-

gallon steel drum that was used to collect trash. I was supposed to visit each site each day and empty the barrel into the
bed of the truck. Then I would pick up around the site and
notice if anything was broken.

When the truck was full, I was to proceed to the dump,
spilling nothing on the way, and return to the task immediately. Gasoline was being rationed at that time, so truck mile-
age was something that needed conserving. If I could figure
out a better way of doing it, he would thank me.

Actually I was able to double the productivity of the truck
by noticing that there were very few picnics during the week.
(As I said, the great discoveries are usually obvious.) So we
did no pickups on Tuesday, Wednesday, and Thursday. On
Monday and Friday I would make a complete tour and perhaps fill the truck up one time. Saturday and Sunday required multiple trips in order to keep the barrels ahead of
the picnickers. Picnic sites and empty buildings have something in common along this line. If someone tosses a rock
through a window, and the window is not immediately replaced, the rest of them will be smashed in a few days. If trash
is permitted to lie on the ground at a picnic site, everyone will
toss stuff in the same location. People think you don't care, I
guess. But my idea worked, and, for a while, I had some extra
time.

As a result, I was given the additional task of delivering
firewood to the various cabins. This involved developing a
new system, and it kept me busy all summer. Other boys my
age were also working there, but under a rigid system that
made it seem to me to be more like the chain gang. One supervisor trusted his people; the other didn't. The results
were obvious.

Job descriptions are usually thought of as something for
the lower-level people in an organization. Higher-ups have
"mission statements" which sound good but are hard to measure. So we have all these people doing things which we may
or may not have agreed to do. It doesn't take very long before a great deal of the organization's work has very little to
do with the main objectives of the business.

If people are going to perform their assigned task, then they obviously have to know what it is, how to do it, and how to measure the results. Either someone has to explain it all to them or they have to figure it out themselves.

In team sports the coaches lay everything out and then teach the players their individual roles. Players are assigned to specific tasks according to their physical ability and other talents. Selecting the right person for the right job is the largest part of coaching. But in athletics it is somewhat easier to know if people are qualified. Physical size, speed, mental quickness, and conditioning are fairly obvious things. The hidden component is "heart," that determination within the individual that may never reveal itself until the right pressure is applied. Coaches learn to sense that in advance but are often wrong, in both directions.

Players in all sports spend their entire careers on the fundamentals. They must learn them over and over. They practice doing the same things until most of the actions are natural. Then they do it some more. When they get too old, or too injured, to perform those basics, they become ex-players.

In the world of organizations, though people are shown the basics quickly when they arrive, they spend the rest of their careers working on other things. They are expected to be properly educated in all aspects of what the organization does and receive new information only when their job changes. There really is little consideration given to the reliability of their competence.

Completely.   The measurement of job performance in most jobs is subjective, revolving around energy, attitude, and output. The only ones who are compared objectively are those in direct production, and that isn't always accurate. This lack of measurement is not due to the absence of data; it is due to the absence of tradition. Managers just aren't used to that sort of thing and don't really know what to look for.

Measurement for my Oglebay boss was easy when the picnic ground was all my job entailed. He just toured the areas looking for the presence of what I was supposed to remove. If any piece of anything was laying about, it was my problem. But when my work was expanded into the firewood business, many more factors came into being. It was not just the presence of firewood where it had been ordered, but the on-time delivery and the attitude of the deliverer in any relationships that might occur with the occupants of the cabins. There was also a keeping of accounts so that the renters could be charged the proper amount on their bills.

Doing the job completely now began to involve many aspects that were beyond his normal way of doing business. So he reverted to his own definition of the basics: the presence or absence of complaints—from anyone. And there were many opportunities: the lady who took the firewood orders, the worker who chopped the wood, the cabin renters, the crew who cleaned the cabins, the accountants who prepared the bills, the park management, and himself when it came to the cleanliness of the truck.

Suddenly I went from being the bright young man who had figured how to cut the picnic trash work in half to the incompetent who could never get the wood to the people on time and was forever marking down the wrong things in the wrong books. In struggling to overcome this, it never occurred to me that I wasn't supposed to know how to do all these things instinctively. I just assumed, as did everyone else, that any dummy should know it all. It finally worked itself out.

The following summer I was home on leave from the Navy, and the boss introduced me to the young man who was taking the picnic clean up and wood distributing job. He was just starting that week. In the next 10 minutes I told him what it had taken me most of the summer to learn. He reported to me later that he never really needed to know anything more than I had explained and as a result had a wonderful season. They all thought he was a lot smarter than I was, and he worked there for years.

The difference between a mediocre career and an outstanding experience is the concept of doing the job completely. Completeness requires that all aspects of the task be understood. Not just "what I do" but "where does my raw material come from," and "what does someone else do with what I produce." The answers to these questions produce the real-life measurements necessary to assure progress. The measurements come into being because people want them, not because of some program developed by management.

When these conditions exist, it becomes possible for people to begin routinely doing things right the first time, which brings us to the next part of the phrase.

At the Correct Time.   Timing is everything in sports. It is why the golf professionals swing so effortlessly and send the ball on a fly 280 yards, while the amateurs swing with all they have and are lucky to attain a score under 200. Some of timing is a gift, but most is learned through diligent work and concentration.

Timing is everything in management too. A reputation for integrity is earned only through doing what one has agreed to do, doing it on time and with completeness. Just being honest is not enough. Honesty is mostly not doing things that are dishonest and is more or less expected of respectable people. Integrity, though, is built up block-by-block through planned employee and management actions based on processes and procedures that are completely understood and agreed upon. Training, internal communications, corrective action, and similar positive tools are considered routine. So is doing things right.

Which brings us to the last of the considerations.

Each of These Tasks to Be Just Exactly What Was Needed to Be Done at the Proper Moment.   Management has to orchestrate the organization so people can know what to do when the ball is snapped, the flag is dropped, or the whistle is blown. If they don't do it, who will? An organization can help itself in accomplishing all this by working on quality improvement through defect prevention. I refer the reader to *Quality without Tears* for more information on that subject. If a company wants to change, it has to conduct a formal education and implementation effort in order to build a process. But the essential ingredient is executive integrity. When the big boss just will not tolerate shoddy performance and is a personal example of what should occur, then the company has a chance. As quality management consultants we learned very early that there is no use even bothering with a management team that was not willing to take on that role.

Managers are struggling with the problem of quality, trying to produce products and services that satisfy their customers and do it with maximum productivity. The media and the quality control experts continually talk about quality control, quality assurance, quality circles, Pareto's analysis, acceptable quality levels, sample inspection, statistical quality control, SPC, and such. These are valuable techniques when used as part of the control process. That is their intended use.

All these become the wrong stuff if the goal is to eliminate the problems of quality. That has not happened in the 45 years of their application.

The reason quality is a problem rather than an asset lies in the management policy and style of the company, not in the tools of measurement and control. Prevention is essential in order to eliminate the agony of nonconforming products and services.

Quality control is to quality management as accounting is to financial management. They are entirely different subjects run by entirely different people. Quality control and accounting keep track and control. Management is policy and action. They need each other but have different objectives and approaches that have little in common.

Quality control and accounting both provide data and regularity, which serve as an information base for quality management and for financial management, respectively. But the application of quality control principles to management action is counterproductive.

For instance, consider the Pareto principle. This says that 80 percent of the events are caused by 20 percent of the items. So in a church 20 percent of the people will donate 80 percent of the money. Anyone who ever served on a church board will know that this is true. In a problem situation, if all the causes are listed, and the frequency of each determined, it will turn out that 20 percent of the causes produce 80 percent of the problems.

All this is so. However, in quality control the analysis proceeds further and divides the distribution into the "vital few" (the 20 percent) and the "trivial many" (the 80 percent). As a result, the 20 percent command corrective action attention and resources, while the trivial many are considered not worthy of attention and are soon forgotten.

Forgotten, that is, by everyone except the customer. These are the items that drive customers nuts and costs up. It is also an open display to the people that management is not taking quality seriously and has resigned itself to mediocre performance. Now both customers and employees are unhappy.

I went to a 30-year retirement party for a colleague recently. He and I were quality engineers together. As one old friend after another spoke, it became clear that there was only one theme: nothing had changed in that company over the past 30 years as far as quality was concerned. The amount of defects was still the same, waivers and deviations were the main business of the quality department, customer complaints were still being handled urgently, and managers still talked about how they loved quality but did all the things that showed they were not serious about it.

The quality professionals have been holding their fingers in the dikes all these years, keeping the company's head above water. They have fought for the company's honor on a daily basis. Their management continually places schedule and cost above quality and views integrity as a trade-off. That is the conventional wisdom of quality.

That American quality has been as good as it has is directly due to the efforts of the quality control people, with little help from operation executives and virtually none from top management. It is not practical to expect more from quality control.

If management wants to produce defect-free products and services on time for its customers, managers have to get serious about prevention. Everyone in the company has to understand quality the same way, and management has to be the example.

They have to know and practice what I call the "Four Absolutes of Quality Management":

1. *Quality means conformance to requirements.* All the actions necessary to run the company, produce the product or service, manage the money, and deal with the customer must be met as agreed. If managers want people to "do it right the first time," they have to tell everyone clearly what "it" is.

2. *Quality comes from prevention.* Vaccination is the way to prevent disease, and the same concept works in organizations. Training, discipline, example, leadership—all these and more—produce prevention.

3. *Quality performance standard is Zero Defects (or defect-free).* This is a clear way of saying "conformance to requirements." In quality control the standard is "acceptable quality level," which means a resignation to a certain amount of errors. This is silly; it would not be tolerated in financial management.

4. *Quality measurement is the Price of Nonconformance.* Manufacturing companies spend at least 25 percent of sales doing things wrong; service companies spend at least 40 percent of their operating costs on the same wasteful actions. (Half the white-collar people are working on old things at any given moment.)

Companies reflect the standards of their leaders, and the tools of quality control will not alter those standards. Permanent improvement requires three phases:

1. The conviction by senior managers that they have had enough of quality being a problem and want to turn it into an asset.

2. The commitment that they will understand and implement the Four Absolutes of Quality Management. They

have to accept the responsibility for making this happen. The quality department cannot do it.

3. The conversion to that way of thinking on a permanent basis. This replaces the conventional wisdom that caused the problem in the first place.

It takes several years to go from conviction through conversion, but improvement escalates from the day the process begins. Management has its future in its own hands. It is not the laws of probability or statistics that have kept managers down, it is their own policy of "that's good enough."

Others have successfully changed. They have the same people, same equipment, same suppliers, same customers— but now they have Zero Defects instead of constant turmoil.

There is no better opportunity for a young up-and-comer than being able to help management change the company around. The key things to remember are

- People will take quality just as seriously as the management takes it, no more.

- Integrity is unrelenting; it can't be done in short bursts of enthusiasm stemming from regret.

- The tools of quality control are not designed to cause prevention throughout the organization.

- Think about quality improvement in terms of earnings per share. A well-established process will double it.

- Every individual in the company needs continual education concerning his or her role in getting things done right the first time and clear requirements on the changing scene within which we live and operate.

4

Growth Is Profitable and Steady

In 1066 William the Conqueror and his Normans invaded Britain. Since they were experienced warriors and had the larger army, they had little difficulty acquiring this land and its people. William believed he was the rightful king anyway, having been promised the title by Edward the Confessor, a belief that has sparked nine centuries of controversy, research papers, and careers. William also believed that the present king, Harold, had reneged on a promise to hand the country over, instead taking the throne himself. The Normans were deeply involved with that land; in fact the just-deceased Edward had been raised as a Norman. Their long-range plan had been to take over Britain for some time. Peaceful means having failed, they brought 1400 ships and proceeded with their hostile takeover.

Actually the country was invaded from Norway at almost the same time William was preparing to move across the Channel. Harold (the king) destroyed the army coming from the north but had expended his resources by the time he faced William. He had little left to fight the takeover and fell on the field of battle along with his staff.

William had the support of many people and wanted to properly reward them when the land was his. The current aristocracy was removed or killed, and the new court prepared to take over the assets. There were no investment bankers involved, so William really had no idea what the Anglo-Saxon balance sheet looked like. However it was obvious that this was an underdeveloped nation that could be made into something by a dedicated management.

So William commissioned the creation of what has been known as the *Doomsday Book.* Each and every article of value was tabulated, from sheep to slaves to wagons. Then the members of the new gentry dispersed it among themselves, leaving little for the natives, who had had nothing under the previous administration either. It takes a long while for the anger created by a hostile takeover to disperse at the senior levels. But usually nothing much changes for the lower groups except that a few are sacrificed one way or another. For the survivors, their "life of quiet desperation" goes on much as before. The new leadership treats them no better or worse than the previous. Although many words are spoken about them, little consideration is offered. There are no serious plans for developing the underutilized talents and potential skills of the people. Facilities, yes; people, no. The Normans built castles everytime they stopped for lunch, or so it seems. They didn't plan to trust their new subjects.

The Norman invasion was necessary for that organization just as continuous expansion and growth is an obligation today. Companies (and nonprofits, too) have to grow if for no other reason than to accommodate the increased expenses that develop over the years. Inflation also raises the cost of everything, and retaliatory price increases are not always possible. Salaries rise as employees gain seniority. The costs of benefits rises because of their very structure, and it is difficult to take any back, particularly if the enterprise is profitable. Therefore cost eliminations and profit improvement must be conducted on a continuing basis, and the revenues of the organization must continue to increase in order to broaden the base.

And, of course, management wants to look good. There is nothing more discouraging to shareholders or the public than a "flat" performance. They just can't stand it when this year's revenues match last year's, even if the profit is up a bit. They want improvement and they want at least 10 percent, with 20 being even more desirable. Hardly anything grows at that rate all by itself, except new companies, and that soon wears off.

Management teams calculate all the ways of making this happen and usually conclude that acquisition is the most rapid and reliable method. When a company is purchased, its known revenues, profits, and assets come along with it. So the financial parts of both companies can blend together with a positive result. Should they bring a loss to the wedding, then it can be deducted against taxable income. A profit adds to what is already accumulated. The short-range benefits are usually positive, which makes acquisitions look like a good idea at the time. There are also some long-range negatives such as incurring debt, or dilution if we pay for it with stock, and the problem of booking "good will" if the price paid is more than book value.

The trouble begins when the new company tries to manage what it bought. That is why the Normans built so many castles to keep the acquired on the other side of a wall. Getting all the people to work together whether they want to or not is where the deal becomes sticky. People worry about their jobs, families, and other basics. They think that the resident staff will suffer if any economies of scale are made. They know that those who will be making the consolidation decisions do not know them and have a loyalty to the home organization.

A balance sheet does not begin to tell the story of a company. There is nothing about people in the *Doomsday Book* the bankers have put together. They concentrate on assets, synergy, spinoffs, consolidations, and such. The people are lumped together as "compensation" and perhaps examined by age in the section on pension liabilities. There is no specific plan for what to do with the acquired employees. The inevitable assumption is that those who did the acquiring are smarter and more competent than those who were swept up. So when the spoils are divided and it is found that there are too many people, guess which group is sent to Scotland to become sheepherders, us or them?

Marriage between two people is at best a 50:50 shot. The successful ones create so much good that it is still worth the effort to try. But in a marriage both people usually walk in with their eyes open; there are very few "takeover" marriages. Everyone gets to vote. When companies join together, only the Boards decide and the individuals involved in making that decision are usually well protected in case they are found to be obsolete.

In any merger a dangerous wedding night is created by the premise that the new management will run the operation more efficiently than the old one. They think that the old management is not taking advantage of obvious opportunities, and that certainly is a possibility. But usually the thinking is that the sum is greater than the parts because of eliminating duplication and taking advantage of common aspects. Executives like to bring together companies that seem to be similar, that have the same customers, for instance. Airline, car rental, hotel, travel service, and credit card companies sound like a marvelous mix. However, although the customer may be the same person, the businesses are exceedingly different. What the customer expects and needs from each of those organizations is quite different and requires an entirely different group of management skills.

The airline takes the customers from here to there and perhaps has them in tow for several hours. The airline customer has to be obedient, reporting to gate 6 at 11 a.m., showing tickets to anyone who asks, buckling up on command, eating what is supplied, and being patiently good-willed about it all.

The hotel customer has a great deal of choice and exercises it within the hotel. Stays of several days are common, and the customer expects constant attention, several eating options, and continuously clean everything—in essence a support system that takes the place of home. Ordinarily there are several hotels to choose from nearby, so guests do not have to put up with anything that makes them uncomfortable.

The rent-a-car customer is seen for a few hurried but brief moments at each end of the relationship. The customer is interested in minimum hassle and a car that gives zero trouble. Major car rental companies all have their counters side-by-side in an airport, the prices are essentially the same, and all have attractive people writing contracts. Others are off the airport, cheaper, just as attractive, and eager to come pick up the customer. Also, much of the business of car rental lies in selling the vehicles after their time is up. So the service-oriented executive can run a completely happy ship only to find no profit at the end owing to a depressed used car market.

Travel service organizations deal with clients on a personal basis, even with package tours. They have to know all the possibilities and cannot be limited to the parent company's hotels and airline. This personal attention given to understanding the client's needs and putting it all together in a bundle is the heart of that business. Unlike in the airline and rent-a-car businesses, the client and the expert spend a lot of time talking about travel arrangements. But clients then take the package and go off to implement it on their own.

Credit card organizations are all paperwork; no one ever sees a customer face-to-face. The entire business wraps around finance rates and "float," which is the money collected or the traveler's checks sold. The main contact occurs when the monthly bill arrives. Credit card companies place some advertising in the envelope. The arrangement is negative all around. Nobody loves those they owe.

The only thing these businesses have in common is money. Travel services and credit cards are cash-flow creators, while the others are capital-intensive. The rent-a-car business rises or falls on the used car market, advertising, location, and rates. Hotels generate a lot of money, but many of their components, such as restaurants, operate in the red. Actually there is one other thing these businesses have in common: they have problems keeping weekend cash flow flowing.

All these companies would probably do better on their own than as part of a network. It is unusual, for instance, for managers to go from one to the other. Years of running a restaurant do little to prepare one for managing an airport car rental location. Staying in hotels while learning the travel agent business teaches nothing about running the place. So the businesses may support each other in some related way, but they do not grow executives for the total firm. For this reason they do not necessarily attract broader-minded people.

If a company concentrates on examining its customers and the needs they express, then the company can grow as it helps the customers be successful. Each business changes enough in itself to keep those who know it best struggling each day to keep ahead of it. Nothing is like it used to be and probably never was.

Just about any business provides endless opportunity for growth; hardly anyone has 100 percent of everything available. There are a lot of strategies for growing within something we already know how to do. It is a matter of understanding the ebb and flow of the business. The secret is in there somewhere; the employees and customers know it and will share if asked.

Strategy is one of the most overworked words in the management vocabulary. It means different things to different people. But for our purposes it should relate to laying out an action plan for the future that commits the money, facilities, and people of the company and contains a goal that can be understood by all. The most important aspect is that it be a practical plan that people are going to take seriously and cause to happen.

Many times managers read long-range plans, nod in agreement, and then wait for something to begin. For instance, when companies begin their Quality Improvement Process, which is a complete strategy of changing the management culture, many folks will be concerned early that nothing is happening. They expect the process to do it all by itself.

They think that educating people, forming teams, and having meetings starts some sort of mystic plasma flowing. They don't realize immediately that management has to lead, and in some cases drag, people along. Constant encouragement has to be given and consistent enthusiasm displayed.

One group was disappointed that it was not receiving many Error Cause Removal (ECR) suggestions from its people. The typical input we see is better than 100 percent because everyone loves to be able to identify the problems that are keeping them from doing defect-free work. This unit had submitted six ECRs from a population of 543. I asked them where the blank forms were kept, and they replied that the boss's secretary had them on her desk. This was considered a central point: anyone wanting one only had to go into her office and ask. I suggested that the six who had done so should be considered for promotion to other work that required bravery. Now the one-page forms are in boxes all over the company, and the biggest problem is keeping up with the flow.

Strategies have to begin with an understanding of what the business consists of, what the ingredients are, what the opportunities are, and where the problems lie. When those are out in the open, the concept begins to reveal itself. Then people who know how to operate the systems and are up-to-date on the world can get at it. Often it helps to have an outside subjective influence to keep the determination on the track.

Consider the case of an insurance company that is bursting with the desire to grow but has not been able to make it happen. In fact things are going the other way. As a result of this concern, the president asked five executives to go off-site for the weekend to work on the strategy. For the sake of simplicity, and my memory, we will name them by their assigned function: Finance, Marketing, Actuarial, Investment, and Production.

The Yearning Insurance Company has had a yearly income growth of 8 percent for the past three years. Currently it is looking at 6 percent, and the future does not reveal much more. The company's beginning was based on life insurance covering the mortgage holder on residences and expanded into comprehensive coverage of everything about a home. All selling was done through company agents, and most of their contacts came from savings and loans or other mortgage companies.

In the past few years the market had been transformed by the growth of single-parent families; people who were single, period; DINKS (double income, no kids); and older folks who didn't have a mortgage or much disposable income. As Marketing put it, "Nothing is like it used to be. We are losing agents every week. They are working in malls, selling to people who came to shop for other things."

PRESIDENT: How many have we lost?

MARKETING: Actually it has been only about a dozen, but the pattern is forming, the pattern is forming.

INVESTING: The decline in interest rates is making it harder to hold our earnings, and the real estate market is a mess. It is a wonderful time to buy things, but income is not something that is part of the wonderfulness.

FINANCE: The cash flow is not as fluid as it used to be. We try to make the claims and expenses come out to about the same as the premiums and make money on investing the cash flow. But there are continual hiccups. Interest rates are down, and we have some empty buildings because of regional economic distress.

PRODUCTION: The amount of paperwork the government wants has increased; the changes the clients continually make are on the increase; our employees are becoming more expensive and less productive; and these new computer systems are very costly, but I don't know how we can get along without them.

MARKETING: We have always had these kinds of problems. Where we are really in trouble is the double whammy we face out in the field. Our traditional market is shrinking with no effort being made to broaden it, and the cost of sales is rising. We have a great string of well-trained agents out there, but it is getting harder for them to make a living. And they are our real customers.

PRESIDENT: Actuarial, you might as well pile some more on this dismal grouping.

ACTUARIAL: If I were a betting woman, which I am not, I would say that our premium rates are going to fall in the next few years. That is because new death rates will be used, based on

10 or so years ago rather than 25 as they are now. This means that while the premium-to-claim ratio will continue as it is, there will be less actual cash passing through our hands.

PRESIDENT: So we haven't even sat down properly, and we are already learning that our market is shrinking, our investments are not paying off as before, our cash flow is sluggish with real hazards in the future, and our clients are living longer, which a good-news–bad-news story.

PRODUCTION: Don't forget the paperwork and computers.

PRESIDENT: Thanks, I was hoping they had gone away. Now here is what I have laid out as an agenda. It is just a beginning, and we can change it to anything you all want. But we are going to spend the weekend here doing whatever it takes to develop a new strategy for this company. Then we will go back and meet with the operating people and get their input. Nothing is going to happen if they can't make it happen. The Board is interested in raising our growth to 15 percent a year with profits to match, and Board members recognize that achieving such a goal may take a while. But they plan on being in business for a long time. We need to be pointed in the right direction. In preparation for this session I sent you the reports that were prepared on our current status and the trends in the industry. Everyone is nodding, so that must mean we have absorbed them. Okay. Let's go over the agenda quickly and get to work. Finance, how about you reading it?

FINANCE: Right. There are only three items: first is "mission," second is "concepts of attaining it" and third is "who does what." I suspect that if we can provide clear answers to the questions those items raise, we will be making a significant contribution to the future of the company—and our own as well.

PRODUCTION: Every time I hear the word *mission* I think of a big, complicated, political-sounding document that everyone nods about but no one takes seriously.

PRESIDENT: We need something everyone can understand.

MARKETING: Something we can hang up on the walls and people can remember.

PRODUCTION: And actually do something about.

ACTUARIAL: How about "to make 12 percent after tax each year"?

PRODUCTION: Somehow I think the Board had something higher-sounding in mind; that would be pure money lust.

FINANCE: They would be happy with that result, but it isn't much of a mission statement.

ACTUARIAL: I realize that, but I would seriously like to hear one that someone uses now, one that people actually live with everyday. Then we would have a model to work with.

PRESIDENT: I remember one mission statement that still sticks with me. It was when President Kennedy said: "We will land a man on the moon and bring him back safely before the end of this decade." That was pretty clear.

INVESTMENT: Clear, but short-term. The space program has sort of wandered along since that time. When the Apollo goals were achieved, it moved along to the Shuttle. But there is no long-range goal that everyone is working toward, like "populate space," or "bring the income tax to Mars."

FINANCE: You're saying that the mission has to be bigger than one task?

INVESTMENT: Right. Suppose we were to select the "earn 12 percent after tax" goal. It isn't really a mission statement, but if people took it seriously, then every decision would be made on that basis. Anything that detracted would not be done. We would be considered money-grubbing-oriented only.

ACTUARIAL: Well at least it would be measurable, not like "go out and do good" or something vague and high-sounding.

MARKETING: This could go on a while, and I know it is really important, but let me just toss in one other thought. Can we go buy another company that meshes with us? I have a couple in mind. All we do is take their tapes, combine their marketing system with ours, and we have increased assets, cash flow, and clients.

PRODUCTION: What about their staffs? Won't they raise our overhead a good bit?

FINANCE: Most of them become redundant.

PRODUCTION: Redundant?

ACTUARIAL: They get fired.

PRODUCTION: Oh.

PRESIDENT: Before we go take on someone else's troubles I think we need to take a look at what our customers are telling us. There has to be a message right in there. The only way to grow properly is to provide something that someone is going to buy and keep the cost of doing that a little lower all the time. We need to go back and examine our business concepts.

FINANCE: Well, insurance is a refined gambling operation in that we bet the customers will let us invest their money long enough to produce the funds to pay them back, or off.

ACTUARIAL: We get to set the odds, but competition wipes out the upside advantage.

PRODUCTION: Our mission is to provide the homeowner with the full protection of insurance, offer competitive rates, and do it all so efficiently that we can make money off the investment portfolio.

PRESIDENT: That's pretty clear. Have you been thinking about this subject?

PRODUCTION: I have, but what I just said came out of the company manual. Apparently it has been there for years but no one ever did much about it. My secretary called it to my attention when she saw the subject of this meeting.

MARKETING: It is pretty much what we should be doing and used to do. However, I think the objective has changed; now the emphasis seems to be on growth, and growth for its own sake.

PRESIDENT: Apparently we are off the track as a company, we don't need any clearer mission than the one we have had. As I think about it, I can see that we have gotten away from those basics and that is where our puzzlement has originated. We don't need a special growth plan; we just need to provide our customers with protection, be competitive, and do it all efficiently.

FINANCE: We haven't been paying as much attention to the salespeople. They provide the personal service that makes the difference. Apparently we are not different from all the other insurance companies.

MARKETING: We are impersonal.

PRESIDENT: OK, I think we are on the path. Let's lay out the concepts of growing through the basics. We'll meet with the operating people and see what they think on Monday.

"Growing through the basics" is going to turn out well for Yearning. They had become sidetracked. They needed to get the key aspects of growth back in their minds:

- Grow where the business is; don't try to make a market where none exists.
- Keep close to the customer's needs.

- Don't assume "a good manager can run anything."
- Don't load the producing people down with nonproductive chores like administrative reports.
- Debt is not your friend.

5

Customer Needs Are Anticipated

Certainly the customer comes first. Who doesn't know that? Ask any executive of any business "Who comes first?" and the reply will resound through the halls: "The customer, of course, dummy. Who else?"

Who else indeed? This is one of the great myths of our time. In reality everyone else comes first if we are thinking of a customer in terms of the one who lays down the money for what it is we are selling. There are many other customers along the way who drain off the intensity of devotion to the final user. It is a matter of the way organizations are run. Staffs are primarily concerned about themselves and what is happening to make their world successful. Real customers can be a bore. In case there is any doubt about this, just keep track of how often concern for this customer is expressed in company meetings. Twice a month would be a lot.

Senior executives of public companies pay more attention to financial market thought leaders than to customers or staffs. Analysts live by the quarter and would prefer to do it by the hour. At a recent meeting one of them asked me how old I was and I said, "241 quarters." The analyst was not amused. This shallow way of looking at things places companies in the position of having to perform continually with upward being the only acceptable trend. One off period and the past is forgotten.

This makes it difficult to plan for the future; no, that is not correct: it makes it impossible to plan for the future. The future requires the expenditure of money, and that means expenses might be higher for a while. In turn, that might lower reported earnings for a moment or two. To people who can read only one number—earnings per share—this means we have hit an iceberg. They lower their lifeboat and head for somewhere else.

So those who run the companies find themselves with many "customers" who affect the state of the organization in different ways:

- The financial community, which is short-range "What-have-you-done-for-me-lately" oriented, and expects only upward trends forever
- The staffers of the company, who expect to be employed, loved, developed, and left alone all at the same time
- The dealers, distributors, agents—if applicable—to whom the company really sells
- The real customers, who come by the company's product or service through the spending of money and decide on a personal basis if they like it or not

If the "real" customer is continually satisfied to the extent of preferring to do business with the company, then all the rest can be handled. So the long-range strategy and the operating policies of the company must direct themselves to that group. Theirs is the only positive influence; the others are all essentially negative. Success comes from customers, not evaluators.

We need to address all this in two particular concerns: first, getting the organization interested in the using customer; and second, figuring out what that person or group of persons wants. If we can clearly aim our effort at genuine customer identification and satisfaction and combine that with actually knowing what their needs are, we will stand a good chance of being eternally successful.

Identifying the customer is not always that easy. When I decided to begin PCA, the advice I received all dealt with how to communicate with and sell to quality control management. However, having been one of those for years, I knew that they had three deficiencies that would keep them from being good customers: they had no power; they have very small budgets; and they think $200 is a lot of money.

We aimed the company at the senior executives because they had the problem, realized how big it was, and expected to make a reasonable investment of time and money in order to get it resolved. The professionals in any area hardly ever come to that conclusion unless their department is headed by someone who is not one of them. To this day many quality control professionals do not think there is much wrong with quality that a few more inspectors wouldn't cure.

So if one picks the wrong customers, examines them carefully to determine their needs, and then delivers the exact requirements—it will all come to naught. The situation or problem will not change, and the supplier's efforts will be viewed as failures.

Toy manufacturers know that adults buy the toys, but children are the real customers. The children are the ones who feel the need and excel at turning their parents, or better yet grandparents, into purchasing agents. Placing an advertisement about robots that turn into automobiles in the New Yorker might not reach this real customer. But Saturday morning TV is another story. And if you can hear the words in the Wheaties cereal commercials, they wind up with "Go tell your momma what the big boys eat." Not too many mothers buy Wheaties cereal for themselves.

Everything is not that simple, of course; but then the thought that children have something to say about the products they use is not that old. It probably came about with the commercialization of radio. Prior to that time, it was hard to reach someone who couldn't read and never went anywhere. The customer for everything was considered to be the one with the purse strings. I suspect the Sears Roebuck catalog opened more eyes than anything before or since.

We have a copy of the 1902 Sears catalog. It is not difficult to imagine a turn-of-the-century rural family sitting with that giant book and beginning to learn what wonderful things were available. Each family member could go over the sections that applied to him or her and select or just dream. Most of the articles were available in a town somewhere or could be ordered through a store. But in a store one had to go find it, and to do that one had to know it existed. In that was the genius of the catalog. It trained the customers to deal with Sears on things they didn't even know they couldn't live without.

Catalogs have changed dramatically since that time. The idea of having one supplier for everything is gone; they are mostly specialized now. The secret here is to identify the customer by finding mailing lists that deposit the catalog right into their hands. Anyone was happy to get a Sears catalog, and people usually wore it out. It was a dream factory. Our house receives 40 to 50 different catalogs a month, which may result in one or two orders for something special. The rest get tossed.

If Sears relied only on its catalog, the way it did in the first third of the century, it would still be a small company. Instead Sears kept up with the changes of its customers, who have a way of slipping off. There is some concern about whether the large regional stores are the way to go now; people are showing signs of wanting to return to small specialty shops with personal service. And TV shopping is becoming a viable way to do things. It could be that family members will huddle around the TV to choose their essentials, the way they did around the Sears catalog, but I doubt it. There are so many choices today that customers can change their way of doing things overnight. Downtowns are becoming popular now that the regional malls are found to not be intimate.

We all know that nobody's customers stay put. They keep

shifting about as their resources, feelings, and attitudes change. That is, of course, what the entire society is about. Things like drunk driving have become socially unacceptable and are in decline. Heroin is falling off among the poor, while the well off are using cocaine. It is very hard to keep up, even on that side of the economy.

And that is precisely the point of this part of the ESO equation. There is no way to anticipate what people are going to do when it concerns their buying and social habits. They don't even know. Trendsetters can be identified and observed, but even they will fall out of step now and then. Each year seasoned and brilliant people get together to produce a Broadway show that lasts one night. I know of no one in the book business who can tell what people will buy.

When The Coca-Cola Company did extensive testing that compared a new flavor with the traditional Coke soft drink, there was a clear preference for the new one. On that assumption, the company tossed the old and brought in the new. The resulting uproar from customers was so big that it was necessary to restore what became Classic Coke, which is now the best seller in the nation again.

My thought is that the wrong assumption was made from a question that addressed the wrong consideration. What Coke asked was "Would you rather spend a long romantic weekend in Bermuda with a brand new attractive companion or your mother?" When a preference was expressed for the new they kicked mother out. That was not what the answerers had in mind, and they revolted. "You didn't ask me if I loved my mother best, you asked about a short-term relationship. Mother and I go back to my childhood. How dare you?" To its credit, Coke recognized the inevitable, recovered immediately, and kept its sense of humor. The company didn't deny us "the real thing" in a fit of petulance, as many would have.

Having raised the question of how we keep the customer first among equals, it is only fair to address the solution. This is the single most difficult area in any business; it is the one that determines, more than any other, the success of the operation. Yet it is one of the least attended. Mature companies perform market surveys and agonize over the results, trying to determine what is going on out there. Then they take thoughtful action and miss the target most of the time.

I remember a dishwasher manufacturer who was losing market share. The company's primary market was new installations, so it was working closely with new-home contractors who wanted dishwashers that were inexpensive but still did a good job. "Cost is the major thing," said the contractors. The manufacturer continually worked on taking costs out of its 20-year-old model. Also, the company brightened the face of the machine and even added panels so "decorator colors" could be placed on each one. They brought together a group of contractors and decorators ("Style is the major thing," said the decorators) to help all this happen. However, the market share kept dropping.

Finally the president happened to ask some of the salespeople if they knew why the customers weren't asking for the product. The salespeople said that customers wanted a machine that was quiet and reliable. Ours, they said, was fairly reliable but noisy. The president said that dishwashers were supposed to be noisy and people should operate them at night or when no one was going to be home.

Then having listened to himself say this, he went over to engineering where they had a design that had been turned down several times. It cost them some money to build a new facility in order to produce this machine, but their market share leaped the first year and kept on growing. The cost of making the machine is much lower, and the reliability is better than before. It has been a success in every measurable way. They even raised the price, which had no affect at all on the continued increase in sales.

Management had been listening to only part of its customer base and to none of the employees who actually knew what was going on in the world. A little investigation showed that this project, and its reasons, had been brought up many times but was unable to get past the capital and finance committees who saw no advantage in spending money on something that was losing market share. They had a report that indicated people were eating out so much that they didn't even need dishwashers. A floor had been laid for leaving the business altogether.

The employees who deal with real customers develop a sense of what those customers need or want. If that information can be extracted, it will serve as the base for knowing what is going to have to happen in order to keep the customers happy. I would guess that no one below the executive floor in all The Coca-Cola Company thought it was a good idea to scrap the drink that built the company and was still selling well out in the world.

But how to find out from the employees? I have tried writing memos, giving pep talks, and all the other "boss down" ways with little success. The information has to be withdrawn like blood, and then processed to identify the diamonds that exist among all the other rocks. Senior management and the lower levels of the organization operate on different databases and frequencies. Those have to be brought together by getting management to listen to what these people are saying.

The listening has to be very close. Customers change for many reasons besides the product or its price. They change because the company becomes difficult to communicate with or more complicated or begins to show signs of arrogance. Sometimes it is because the person they have been dealing with goes away. The product, whether tangible or intangible, is not always the key. After all it is hard to tell one bank from another when it comes to products. Some flourish while others fail to grow. There is a lot involved besides how much interest is paid on certificates of deposit. Location, atmosphere, service, employee attitudes, and executive awareness are some of the broad reasons for this difference.

The tellers know why Mrs. Brown moved her account across the street. The design engineer knows why the customer turned down the proposal for the new widget, the accountants know why the Smith Company is always late in paying. It is all there, if one can get at it.

The Sales Trip

"Well Jim," said Harry, "how was your trip? We were very pleased to hear the report that said Hartley and Company will be giving us another order."

"Good trip chief, good trip," said Jim. "It's getting a little harder these days, but I still enjoy being out with the customers."

"All of us slow down a little bit as time moves on," Harry said.

"Oh it's not me. I admit I've learned to travel a little lighter in case I have to carry a suitcase, but I'm not the one who is making it a little harder. It is just the changes in the way customers do things."

"Like what, for instance."

"Well take Hartley. I used to go in and see Mr. Hartley, and we would look over his inventory and make up an order to get it up to the level he liked. Then we would go to lunch, and I would tell him about our new products. If there was anything that interested him, he would call the Engineering and Production guys and I would go see them. If they liked the new products, we would work out a qualification schedule and satisfy them that it was what they needed. We did that every two months, like clockwork."

"That sounds like a great arrangement. It took you a long time to build up that relationship."

"A long time. Now Mr. Hartley is not as active in the business, and I deal with the Materials and Engineering people. They are very professional, but things are a lot different, in what they want, I mean."

"You mean in terms of products? We can send some of our R&D people with you next trip, and they can get in a word with Hartley. We sure don't want to lose them. I'll call Johnson—"

"They are already working with us, chief. That isn't what I'm talking about. Our products do fine; it's our systems that make things harder."

"Get specific," said the boss.

"They don't want inventory any more. They want things

delivered on a regular basis and then moved right to the shop areas. They want to get rid of the warehouse."

"That sounds like a good idea; is it possible?"

"Oh sure, lots of companies do it. Their suppliers have to send them material that is exactly correct and have to have good schedule control. We don't do that. This may be the last big order we get from Hartley if we don't learn how to deliver 'just-in-time' inventory style."

"Our folks don't want to do that? I think we are very up to date."

"Afraid not chief. The production people won't even talk about it, the quality department says it's impossible, and the engineers just shrug their shoulders. We have never worked that way."

"And other customers are expecting the same thing?"

"Absolutely. They all want to reduce the costs and hassle that make them noncompetitive."

"We all want to do that. What's different?"

"They are changing their whole culture—all the stuff we have read about for years, the things that sounded so good but that no one ever did. You know: Zero Defects; employee participation; materials control; well they are actually doing those things now and are very serious about the results. We have to get with it."

"We will. Let me do a little research and I'll get back to you. Tell Hartley that we won't let them down."

Anyone who has been in the business world knows that salespeople sometimes come back with a tale about how what is going on is not their fault. What isn't usually realized is that there is usually truth in the tale. Those who ignore it are doing so at their risk. Business executives have to be like the young swain who is attentive to every mood and interest swing his beloved expresses, no matter how discreetly or modestly they are displayed.

"Why does she seem a little pensive? Have I said something, or did I fail to say something? Was tonight's good night kiss a little shorter than last night's? Can she be losing interest in me? Did she linger a little longer in choir practice last Wednesday evening? Do I have a competitor? Could it be that George Watson? He's just back from a big eastern college and is probably more interesting than me. I need to read more."

And on and on.

Organizations need to worry about their customers in the same way. "It's two o'clock. Do you know where your customers are?"

Managers have to interrogate both clients and employees continually. They have to get in and root around. They have to go visit customers and say: "We have come here to listen to you." They have to do the same with employees. The mission of the company has to be continually examined to keep it real, and the work of the company has to be concentrated on accomplishing the mission.

Cooperative customers will help the suppliers who show some interest in continually improving the relationship. And that is what it is all about: relationships. New and exciting products help, as well as innovative pricing and financing. But what binds the supplier and the customer together is the feeling that one will take care of the other if the other takes care of the one.

When a customer's business changes, or the way things are run is altered significantly, then the supplier needs to know that and be ready to help. This doesn't apply just to professional purchasing like between corporations; it fits exactly with the personal purchaser.

I remember when people used to go to several stores to gather all the ingredients of the evening meal for the family. The meat store sold meat, the bakery sold bread, the produce market sold produce, and so on. But the customers decided that they wanted to spend less time running around. The women who traditionally stayed home were finding other things to do that were more interesting and useful than grocery shopping. Many were working; many just wanted more freedom.

So the supermarket was born, and the specialized stores began to disappear. Those who are still around do well because they serve the needs of clients who want special products or treatment. But the entire business changed in only a few years, and it has not stopped yet. Concepts of marketing or selling can become obsolete quickly if the customer is forgotten for a few minutes.

Auto dealers are learning that people want a wide range of choices. So where they used to have one brand of automobile, they are now mixing things up. There is an automobile dealer near our place in Savannah who sells Buick, BMW, Mercedes, Isuzu, and a couple of others. Whatever need you have, they can meet it. If the customer wants a Cadillac, they will get it also. They have become customer-oriented rather than product-based. Some day autos will be sold in a big mall instead of individual dealerships. The maintenance will be a dealership.

The senior managers of any organization have to continually be forced to keep up. Perhaps they should have to find a customer and spend time with him or her each month. Marketing can't do it all by itself, and sometimes the professionals get so close to the trees that they don't know the woods are all around them.

Key thoughts about customers:

- Relationships determine success.

- Today's correct concepts are good only for today.

- Top management should know some customers personally.

- Don't let the internal customers take precedence over those with the real money.

- Advertising should build confidence in the company first and the product second.

6
Change Is Planned and Managed

Ellen Culberston got up from her desk and walked over to the window. She was not pleased with the news Harry was bringing her.

"All that stuff is a passing fancy, Harry," she said. "I have looked into what is really going on, and the business of not having inventory on hand is just not true."

She turned to Harry, and dropped the tone of her voice a bit.

"They store the material in trucks instead of warehouses, they just drive by and drop some off and then go park for a couple of hours. Or they get a storage facility near by and make pickups from there. If something is rejected and sent back, they take it to their place and rework it. I don't believe it is possible to do what you say these people want to do."

Harry waited patiently for her to run down. Ellen really knew production, but she could be stubborn about changing. She needed a great deal of convincing to recognize that something was broken enough to fix. This was not going to be an easy matter.

"I know you think that what we are doing is the extent of what can be done, but believe me there are a lot of changes going on out there. Our customers want us to do something different; I think we need to at least find out for sure."

Ellen thought about that for a moment and nodded.

"I don't mean to put up a roadblock about it, and I am willing to be convinced, but we have to deal with reality. Their costs get lower with this type of system, but ours get higher. We wind up financing their inventory."

Harry shook his head.

"Not so boss, not so. You know that I have been working to eliminate in-process inventory in our plants. We have been spending a fortune for years financing it and moving it around."

Ellen turned sharply.

"And we have spent a lot moving machines closer together and rearranging the facilities. I hope you all know what you are doing."

Harry blushed and began to get a little impatient.

"We have cut several hundred thousand dollars so far, but that is only the beginning. And that makes the point I am getting to. We have to be ready to accept the reality of change. We have to continually look at the concepts we use as our operating philosophy."

"This defect-free zero inventory thing is not a fad. It is here to stay, and those who don't make it happen aren't going to play at all."

Thoughtful now, Ellen nodded.

"OK," she said. "I am willing to be convinced. What do you suggest?"

Harry had a plan.

"I thought we could get ourselves invited over to Hartley's to see what is happening. They are the leaders in all this, as far as we know. Having you call on them might also help us when their next order comes up too."

"Let's take Jim with us," said Ellen.

"It's all set; he will be our host. I cleared it with your secretary; we're going Thursday morning. Hartley is even going to take us to lunch. They are delighted that you are coming."

Ellen smiled and returned to her desk.

"I'll see you Thursday then. No matter how it turns out, I am looking forward to my brush with reality."

The company plane took a quick 90 minutes to take Ellen and Harry to a small airport on the edge of town. Jim was waiting to drive them the few miles to the Hartley complex. "We will make it right on time, Ellen," said Jim. "They are all very excited. I am going to drive past the inventory warehouse they just closed, so you can get an idea of how serious they are. Mr. Hartley considers that a personal achievement. Everyone thought he was getting senile." Ellen just looked out the window. Harry and Jim exchanged worrisome glances. This could be a long day.

The Hartley complex covered a lot of ground and seemed to be a forest of one-story buildings. Jim drove expertly through the maze and up to the glass enclosed front of one building.

"Always drive to the flagpole," he smiled. "That's the first thing they teach us in sales 101."

He parked in the visitor's slot, and the three entered the building, looking for the receptionist's desk.

Wilson Everetts, the Materials Director, and Bob Brown, the Systems Integrity Director, came through the lobby door at that moment, and Jim introduced them. The guests signed the registration book and received badges, and the group moved into the hallway.

"We thought you might like to have a little tour to get oriented," said Brown. "Then we will meet Mr. Hartley in the cafeteria for lunch, and after that we will go to the conference room to provide a more formal briefing for you. If there is anything you are particularly interested in, just let us know."

"Sounds great to me as is," replied Ellen. "I always like to see the overall picture before getting into details. How many people do you have in this facility?"

"There are 3240 overall," said Wilson, "and 2635 in the bargaining unit. And we have the corporate engineering group here also. That is about 185 people."

"Business has been strong," commented Bob. "We are beginning to deliver overseas now."

"Yes," smiled Wilson, "and we have had to learn a whole

new thing about materials handling. Packaging for shipment was a big problem. Our first few deliveries were disasters. We just didn't recognize that there had been a change."

"What kind of change?" asked Ellen.

Wilson gestured for them to follow him and led them through a door into a factory area. There were boxes stacked on pallets, and three people were strapping them with wire.

"This wasn't on the tour, but since the question came up, let's look at it. Over here is the package we use to ship our products domestically. It has worked out well for many years. We have virtually no damage."

"But when it came to overseas shipment, we had to deal with a greater potential for physical damage, plus saltwater, plus pilferage, plus some other things. So we had to design a whole new container. This is it over here. As you can see it is actually lighter and smaller, but it is much stronger and easier to deal with."

Harry nodded. Their company (Wellington) was just beginning to become involved in shipping overseas, and he knew that no one was even thinking about the packaging material.

"What we are learning," said Bob, "is that nothing seems to be permanent. Everything has to be reviewed continually. I'm beginning to think that the half-life of an executive is about one month. It takes that long for things to get obsolete."

They went back to the hallway and into the factory operation. The floor was so clean that it reflected their shoes. This was a dramatic contrast to what they were used to seeing at Wellington. All the metal and the walls were painted with bright colors. Harry was impressed.

"No one is walking around," he said.

Bob smiled, "We have tried to work out the jobs so that there is no need for much flow. Since the real-time computer system came in the office, people can get what they want without coming out here every 30 minutes."

"Real time?" asked Ellen.

They stopped before a computer terminal and Wilson asked the nearest worker if she had a moment.

"This is Harriet Askew," said Wilson, introducing everyone. "Perhaps you could show our guests how this terminal works and what we use it for, Harriet. She has had a big part in making this system work."

Harriet smiled at everyone and proceeded.

"At this installation point I check to see if the two previous assemblies are on correctly and then place this plate on the top of the product. If there are any problems, I tap them in on the keyboard here. Let me call up the current status."

She punched a menu key and then another code and a bar chart appeared.

"This shows that there were seven defective mountings during the assembly of the last 1000 units. There also were three shortages of material, all of them this item here, the top plate."

Ellen was interested. She leaned closer to the machine and asked Harriet: "What was wrong with the seven mountings?"

"Work quality. The operator didn't stamp the code number on the side of the unit. I stopped the line each time, and she came on down and did it quickly."

"What will happen now?" asked Jim. "Will she be disciplined or retrained or what?"

"She put in a suggestion that the number be put on when the supplier makes the panel," said Harriet. "The engineer came by this morning and said that is a good idea and it will start with the next order, which will be this week."

Ellen thought about how many months such an action would have taken in their operation. The worker also would have been blamed for the entire problem. This way was much simpler and direct. It had to cost an awful lot of money though. Money was something they were not used to spending at Wellington.

"What I like about all this," commented Bob, "is that I can sit at my desk and monitor the defect rates all through the system, including the office areas. These systems were only for the shops before. I used to have several analysts who did nothing but keep charts and poke around. Now those people are involved only with corrective action. It was one of them who took the suggestion and walked it through the system."

Everetts thanked Harriet, and the group went over to the receiving area. Eight truck bays were operating simultaneously. People wearing coveralls were pushing hand trucks up the bays and moving boxes of material off to the receiving areas. They all seemed to be happy with their work, and there was a sense of purpose about it all.

"Is this where the 'just-in-time' material arrives?" asked Ellen. "What happens to it when they cart it away?"

"Each cart stops by one of the recoding terminals, and the clerk enters what has been received. Then the material is moved to the work area and unpacked so it can be used," said Bob.

"But how about receiving inspection?" asked Ellen. "How do you know the material meets the specifications? Isn't it all rather risky?"

Bob led her over to a terminal that was not being used at the moment and called up some data. The shift was coming to an end, and people were beginning to close the operations down.

"All that is taken care of before it ever gets here. Each supplier has agreed to deliver defect-free material, and we have worked with them, as necessary, to make certain that happens. And they have to do it by prevention, not by adding a bunch of appraisal functions."

Ellen was concerned. She sat down at the terminal expectantly and furrowed her brow.

"I hear what you are saying. We all want that. But how can you be sure it is happening without having a receiving inspection station?"

Bob smiled.

"Everything gets checked eventually as it is put together. When there is a problem, it is reported and shows up right here."

He called up a chart.

"Now we have had these defects. Let's see what they were; I'll call up the list of them."

A list of items appeared showing problems that had occurred during that day's production.

"This is a total list," said Bob, "I can get one on a continual basis during the day. Every time a defect or other problem occurs, we know about it right away. Then we can take action."

"How do the suppliers find out, and what can they do about it at this late date?"

"Well it isn't so late. As you can see, we have very few of them. In fact there were 15 all day today that are supplier-caused, and 10 of those are the same item. According to this, the cause has been identified as 'wrong part.' That probably means that the supplier shipped the wrong configuration. The supplier will have the proper ones by now. We will follow up with the supplier to get a satisfactory answer about what they are going to do to prevent that from happening in the future."

"Have you ever dropped a supplier because of that sort of thing?" asked Ellen. "It would seem to me that it is going to happen once in a while. What do you do if they are a sole supplier?"

"We have dropped several who couldn't seem to get the idea, and we find that sole suppliers are easy to work with. They know that we could produce ourselves if we had to. Along that line," commented Bob, "we have been able to reduce our total supplier base by about 50 percent. Our purchasing costs are lower, but the suppliers find it more profitable for them. We can give bigger orders, and they do less checking since their processes are in control."

Everetts came over, checking his watch, and suggested that they all move on to the cafeteria to meet Mr. Hartley. As they walked along, Ellen noted that everyone seemed to be working. There were no groups standing around trying to solve some problem. This was not something that was routine to her.

Bob was talking about Hartley.

"He is semiretired, doesn't do much about running the company, and nothing about day-to-day operations. He travels, visits other companies, goes to conventions and trade shows, takes courses at the university with his grandchildren, and reads everything he can get his hands on. He really is on top of things and knows right away when a better concept comes along. He also can pick the false ones right out of the person's mouth."

"I'm looking forward to meeting him," said Ellen.

"I've been looking forward to meeting you, Ellen," said Hartley, as they entered the lunch area. "Wellington has been a reliable supplier to us for years and I know for a fact that a large part of that is due to your work. Let me help you with your chair."

The older man moved quickly around the table, and after making certain that everyone was seated, he got them up again.

"I always like to get everyone seated so they can feel comfortable about leaving the table. We are going to the cafeteria lines over there. You will notice that one area is for hot lunches, one for deli, one for salads, and one for 'short order.' We find that this system is much quicker and gives people the choice they like instead of the standard line."

"How long has this been installed?" asked Harry.

Hartley looked at Everetts.

"Three years, Wilson? Something like that. People had quit coming in here; they would bring their own or get something from the machines."

"The executive dining room was eliminated also," said Bob. "It was amazing how much the food improved when the managers started eating here. And everyone likes being able to see them every day too."

Ellen shook her head.

"You people seem to be up-to-date on everything. Are you making changes constantly? Don't the employees get upset with everything being different every day."

Hartley laughed. He was enjoying this.

"We really haven't changed all that much, and we are very careful not to make changes just for entertainment. In fact I can't make any at all myself, but I do make recommendations to the Systems Integrity Board (SIB)."

"Systems Integrity Board?" said Ellen and Harry in unison.

"Now that is a new one on me," said Harry. "I never heard of that Board. What do they do? What are they part of?"

"They keep track of changes, or make them happen."

Ellen looked at Bob.

"Your title is Director—Systems Integrity, isn't it? I was meaning to ask you about that. Are you involved in quality?"

"Yes, part of what I do is what the quality department used to do. We have expanded the concepts and approaches in order to concentrate on prevention."

Hartley raised his hands.

"Wait, hold on. We'll explain it all to you a little later. Let's finish our lunch and then go to the conference room. We have a short presentation on what we are doing and some things we are bringing to the attention of suppliers. After that we can discuss the SIB in detail."

The tape-slide presentation gave a clear description of the quality improvement process that The Hartley Company had installed, and then the hosts laid out the inventory program. It was easy to see that they complimented each other. The actual and projected financial savings were impressive. The new systems clearly paid for themselves and improved income in the process.

"We did not do any of this a few years ago," said Bob, "but what you have seen, and other things, have made a big difference in our business."

"Keeping up-to-date without wearing yourself out or spending into oblivion is very difficult," said Ellen. "You all seem to have done well at it. I would like to know how you tell the good ideas and systems from the bad. How do you know what is going to work?"

Hartley smiled at that.

"We don't always know, but we can find out by approaching change in a planned and positive manner. I have learned that more harm comes from automatically rejecting anything new than from giving it a fair evaluation."

Ellen was thinking about how this concept could apply at Wellington, where change was considered an instrument of the devil. Some hard questions would be asked.

"I still don't quite understand where the initiative for change originates. Is there someone in charge of that?"

"Oh no, but once it becomes apparent that management is actually interested in learning about better ways of doing things, ideas just seem to pour in. That's why it is necessary to do evaluations and analysis."

"What did you do about quality circles?" Harry asked.

"We inquired around enough to get some history and learned that they are very successful when they are part of a management-driven companywide quality improvement process but a disaster when tried on their own. So we didn't do anything with quality circles until our process was working so well that the people just sort of rose up and demanded a better way of communicating on problem solving. Then we started circles to provide it," replied Bob.

"We had to go outside to get help with the quality management process," said Hartley. "It is not possible to teach that sort of change inside a company. It takes a lot of credibility."

"And all the computer programs, you seem to have a broad spectrum of them," noted Ellen.

Everetts nodded.

"That's true. But each has a purpose, and they all have to fit together. We spent some money we didn't need to spend before we learned that they didn't have to be compatible in every regard. But now we have pretty solid real-time and historical data. I really think we would not be able to operate without them."

Ellen smiled at Mr. Hartley.

"You promised to explain Systems Integrity (SI) to us."

Hartley smiled back at her. "SI has made it possible for us to change when we need to and to use what is working when that is best."

"What brought all this about was the realization that a company, being a living, growing entity, was in a continuous state of change just like a person. There is no way to hold it back. So we decided to look at change as being our friend instead of a pain in the neck.

"If we can identify the need for change, as in where something isn't working well, and the opportunity for change, as in where we learn about something that has been developed, and have a positive system of evaluation and control—then we could keep up-to-date or ahead of the competition. That is the beginning of Systems Integrity.

"The secret word, as Groucho used to say, is 'prevention.' Keeping out of trouble instead of learning how to solve every new disaster is the idea. There are a lot of benefits to be gained from preventing."

"We have a paper on it," said Bob, "to explain the nuts and bolts; if you would like I will give it to you before we leave today."

"That would be excellent," said Ellen. "This has been a very worthwhile visit for me, for all of us. It is possible to become complacent without realizing it. We have been concentrating on reducing costs and becoming more competitive, and in the process we may have set ourselves up to become stagnant."

Mr. Hartley nodded.

"That can happen, Ellen," he said. "Our operations were mummified; they were so wrapped up in doing one thing only that they got themselves into trouble. Change is our friend when we manage it; it is a disaster if we just change to change. But we cannot pressure our managers to the point that they avoid it just because it might involve spending some money in order to save money. And, even worse, we could be left behind. I remember a saying I heard somewhere: 'The only difference between a rut and a grave are the dimensions.'"

"We almost did that on quality," said Bob. "We got so involved with the traditional quality control methods we didn't realize that we were committed to always having waivers and deviations. Life is a lot simpler now."

Systems Integrity—
An Overview

Hartley and Company contains an average of 16,000 people, organized into five divisions, which deliver many services and several hundred products. The systems that make Hartley run cover everything from payroll, through sanitation, purchasing, assembly, and marketing, to the dozens of other functions that have to be performed if the company is to operate.

Effectiveness requires that all these systems complement and support each other. Just as a sports team needs each player to work together and communicate in a standard manner, so business must do the same. But when a major league first baseman changes something about his operating method, the other players all see it and are immediately involved. They adjust, or make suggestions, and work it out together.

However, the functions of business organizations encompass many different disciplines. When accountants, for instance, change their way of doing something, it is not obvious to those who are busy in personnel, quality, or some other function of the organization. Yet the altered system is bound to affect the work of these groups. Ordinarily it would be necessary to have a mess before anyone poked around enough to learn that something had changed. Then there would be a scramble, hurt feelings, lost time, disrupted operations, and such.

Organizations traditionally stumble along accepting the situation that their detailed management systems are not compatible. The most promotable executive has always been the one who is resourceful about resolving the problems that happen because of this way of operating. Unfortunately, this is usually the same person who resists formalizing the management of change. One person's adventure is another person's frustration. Change has never been thought of as something that required formalization or, for that matter, could even be handled in a planned fashion.

Manufacturing companies usually have some sort of change board that meets and gives the shop people a chance to tell the engineers their troubles. These sessions concentrate on arranging the orderly implementation of product changes. They were not designed to evaluate suggested changes for worth or to seek out system-oriented alterations.

If a company is going to approach the management of change in a routine manner, several things have to be considered:

1. There has to be a body at the center of it all, and that is the Systems Integrity Board, which is chaired by the Director—Systems Integrity. This board is a group of senior people who usually meet once a month for an hour or so. Proposed changes are brought to them for acceptance or rejection. In addition to the control aspect of this meeting, the most important part is that the attendees are kept up-to-date on what is happening in the running of the organization. Usually they know all about the products and the finances, but little about where all that paper goes or what systems are used to manage the company, except those under their direct control.

2. The operating departments have to be brought together regularly in an Integrity Implementation Committee. Here representatives from all areas meet to put into effect the changes approved by the SIB. The new form, the altered system, the change in philosophy on selecting suppliers—whatever—will all be installed at the same time. Most importantly, those who are doing it will understand what is supposed to happen. This committee will schedule

schooling as well as paperwork. Change is a serious business; it is incredibly expensive to do things wrong and over all the time.

3. The company has to actively examine what is going on in the world and what has been developed. It has to be oriented to the needs of its customers, suppliers, and employees. Managers have to seek out improvement and determine if it would help them. The routine changes will emerge from within the organization; the new concepts will probably originate outside the company.

The Systems Integrity function replaces the regular quality control (QC) operation. Many of the QC activities will need to be conducted under this department, such as statistical process control and supplier evaluation.

However, the attention of the function will be on prevention rather than appraisal, and the scope will be broadened to include all systems of the organization. Internal financial auditing, for instance, should be part of Systems Integrity. The internal audit concept is then expanded to perform regular reviews of the systems that run the company: purchasing, payroll, procedures control, inventory, mailing, marketing surveys, personnel, and everything else.

We are not talking about a big organization, just a few people who more than earn their own way through helping the other functions prevent expensive problems. Companies having quality control functions will find that it takes fewer people to run Systems Integrity, with much more effect. Waivers and deviations will become a thing of the past, and white collar areas will receive the same prevention attention as blue collar. It is the white collar area, after all, where the major opportunities for problem prevention lie.

The three travelers were excited as they made their way back to the plane. Ellen, particularly, was encouraged by what she had learned.

"We are just going to have to get Wellington moving. I think we are sound asleep in several areas. We will bring some folks together and get a plan laid out. Then I am going to invite some Hartley people to come speak to them, after they have rejected my proposal."

Harry was startled.

"What makes you think they will reject it?"

"That is the way we have always done things," she replied. "Didn't I almost throw you out of the office? It is a wonder that we are still in business."

Jim was pleased with the results of the trip also.

"We will get our next order with no problem, but the one after that will depend on how well we are supporting them."

"We will support them," said Ellen. "But don't forget that it took Hartley a while to change. Don't promise them any miracles. For a while we will have to learn to handle change."

The key aspects of change are

- The world keeps on going around whether we want it to or not. Keep looking ahead.

- Not every change is good for us; not every change is bad. Each needs to be evaluated subjectively.

- Managing change means that everyone has to be involved enough to know what he or she will have to do about it.

- Systems Integrity deals with each part of the organization and its relationships with others.

- Watch out for changes recommended eagerly by those would profit from it.

7

People Are Proud to Work There

We all have watched as organizations were transformed from a place everyone loved into one nobody could stand—all in only a few months. Changing love to hate doesn't take very long. Returning from hate to love can require years, if it ever happens, because folks are afraid of being disappointed or hurt again.

The reasons managers work to turn their people against them are not always easily understood. The villains never think of themselves as evil, and the victims are usually ready to assume more than their proper share of the blame. We know from history that when people are locked up they are often heard to sigh: "If only the leader knew what was going on, he would set us free and punish those who did this to us." Little do they know who is behind it all.

But why should business leaders want their employees to hate the place, or at best be uncomfortable there? Why would they tolerate a situation where people do not look forward to coming to work and trample each other in order to not spend one extra moment at the end of the day? Why do they accept the employees getting most of their information by rumor? Why do they permit managers to harass the employees?

The kindest answer is that they do not know it is all going on, which means they are insensitive to the employees. The truest is that they don't care, believing that people should make their own world and are responsible for their own happiness or discontent. The leadership becomes separated from the day-to-day reality that makes up the actual lives of regular people. Executives, in particular, can come to think that because they, personally, have somehow overcome and risen to a level above organized hassle, that others should be able to do the same. Unfortunately there are only so many slots whose natural position is above the fray.

I once had a boss who was very disturbed because he kept receiving complaints about a hotel we owned. He stayed there regularly, he told me irately, and never had any trouble. In fact the hotel people were always extra pleasant and went out of their way to take care of him. I was never able to convince him that he was not receiving routine care. What I did, though, was convince the hotel management that they should treat each customer as though he or she were the boss. (I never did get them to quit calling customers "guests." Guests have to do what you want to do; customers can call the tune.)

The organization that people are proud to work for earns that honor through consistent relationships and can lose it with very little effort. It is not a matter of money, charm, or benefits. They are important in their way, but a great deal more is involved. I have never been treated so poorly as I was during military basic training, yet we were all very proud of our unit. We received no respect and no benefits, had no voice in what was happening, and were constantly reminded of our worthlessness. But we would fight for our anthill, should someone make light of it.

I know companies where the employees are treated to every benefit and consideration that the Human Resources Administration can create. The company is generous, not only with money, but with promotions, education, travel, and counseling. There is a system of continuous evaluation, where the employees rate the company and where the company rates the employees. No one ever gets laid off, although the incredibly disruptive can get fired, with proper severance of course.

Most of the people appreciate what the company does for them but do not necessarily award respect to it. And pride does not necessarily emerge from all this. There is little to be proud of personally when everything is supplied. It could be like the "poor little rich girl" they make movies about. The people are left with little to accomplish. Many feel like birds in gilded cages, which is ridiculous, but not necessarily inaccurate. Staffers get comfortable; they don't need change. One day they look up and find that their products are becoming obsolete. Perhaps a little suffering is necessary in order to keep our spirits humble and sharp.

I am also familiar with companies which give their employees the absolute minimum in benefits, treat them all with disrespect, and have no consistent personnel policies. The employees despise the management and have zero pride in the business. They look at it only as a meal ticket and would leave immediately if they had another place to go. Everyone who is employable elsewhere has gone. Only those the company deserves are left. The best of conditions would be somewhere in the middle of these management styles.

Executives recognize the importance of pride, of course, and most want their employees to have it. The reasons behind this vary from those who just want the employees to enjoy life more to those who know the company will be more profitable and happy if pride exists. In order to achieve this, many actions are taken. Several companies started PRIDE programs, having constructed the name from something like Personal Reliability Installs Direct Efficiency or Pride Is Really Desirable Everyone.

In one company the employees, recognizing a cost reduction effort when they saw it, renamed the program: Prepare Resumé Immediately, Department Eliminated. They accomplished this by placing a comma between I and D on the hundreds of PRIDE signs all around the company. It took some time for the managers to catch on, and when they did, they saw no humor in it. The signs came down, and nothing has been said on the subject since. Acronyms have fallen out of favor there.

One high-tech company management team decided that it wanted to avoid the problems that seem to come from rapid growth, namely, the loss of team spirit and pride in the company. The downside starts about the time the organization passes 150 employees, according to my unscientific surveys. People have to deal with the professionals instead of the principles, and the crassness of procedural control and impersonal assignment enters the world.

This management was particularly proud of the "open" environment that existed. Employees wore casual clothes, all were apparently equal, and folks would stay around for impulsive "beer busts" after work. It was a wonderful place to work. So the leadership set out to define the culture of the company and lay it out for everyone to see. That way it could be maintained.

They labored for weeks over the definitions that described the culture of the company and then announced them to the people. The reaction was not as positive as expected, and although everyone went through the motions of being enthusiastic, the charter was generally ignored. The president couldn't understand this. It never occurred to him that the announcement saying that the most important thing about the management style of the company was "openness"—had been created in private. A better word would be secret.

The management team had disappeared into its conference room to work on this with no one else participating. All other meetings in the company were held with the doors open and a spoken invitation for anyone who was interested to come in and sit down. The president included this tradition in the speeches he made about the organization. Articles had been published on this and other open practices.

Naturally the office staff began to think that something desperate was going on when the chiefs began shutting the door. They had no idea that the leadership thought it was preparing a happy surprise for the troops. This unsettling awareness began to spread around the company and was later thought to be a contribution to the company's demise. It was at this point that the employees began to lose confidence in the leadership. The really good people start preparing to disappear when leadership begins to have credibility problems. They can get a job anywhere. Each loss of pride produces an exodus that leaves the organization in the hands of the less competent—which is nothing to be proud of.

Changing the unproud to the proud is a complex and unyielding operation. It is much better to start out proud and keep working to improve the feeling, stopping short of arrogance, of course. But organizations can be changed. I had a personal experience with a company that gave me some insight on the subject. Their business would be considered "service," but the situation was similar to that found in many manufacturing plants. The product has little to do with pride, although there are some things people don't admit to making. But then this isn't all true anymore; almost everything is advertised on television now.

The company I have in mind invited me to come visit during a tour I made as part of being chair of the Heart Association fund drive. It had never made a contribution, and the Board felt that I might be able to spark the management since my strategy was just to ask for some money rather than hint around. It is amazing how people will respond when they learn they can purchase their way out of guilt.

But when my guide led me through the office toward the general manager's office, my heart began to sink. The place was a mess. Each desk had piles on paper on it, the filing cabinets were disorganized, and what paper would fit on the desks was on top of them. Scraps of more paper were on the floor. Empty coffee cups were placed casually about. The people were casually dressed, to put it mildly.

"We have a fine group of people," said my guide. "There isn't a more dedicated office in our system."

The general manager, let's call her Helen Winston,

greeted me in her reception area. She looked better than the rest, but her office matched the decor of the main area. It appeared to me that these people were compulsive savers.

"We are delighted to have you visit us. Our entire management team is joining us for lunch. And I have invited some of the key employees too. We will have it in the conference room; it is being sent in. Have you ever been in a company like ours before?"

I replied that while I hadn't dealt with one in their particular field, I was somewhat familiar with it. But since I would like to know more about it, perhaps she would take a moment and tell me about the problems and opportunities that were happening. We obtained a cup of coffee, and I sat on the couch.

"Our biggest problems are getting good people and figuring out what the customers want," she said. "It is very hard to find people who really want to do a good job and who want careers in this field. We pay well, and the future doesn't look bad at all."

I asked about the turnover rate and she said it was 2 percent a month, which is around one-fourth of the people a year, and has to be disruptive. It apparently was not limited to the lower levels; the professionals were coming and going quickly also.

"The customers," she said, "are only price-sensitive. They are going over to the foreign firms that are buying into our business. They all have government funding, so it is very difficult to compete with them."

I noted that customers today seemed much more interested in reliability—that they would receive exactly what had been promised, when it was promised.

"Are these international firms less expensive to deal with than yours? Or others in the field?" I asked.

"We're not absolutely certain," she said, "but that has to be one of the main reasons for customer switches. We have a study going on it. But as for reliability, that is one of my biggest concerns. We talk about it all the time. I have been having sessions with the employees in small groups just to let them know how important I feel quality is."

She smiled and blushed a little.

"I was hoping we might get you to make a few comments on this subject at lunch today. Perhaps hearing it from you would help convince some of them that this is a serious problem. Would you mind?"

I assured her that I never minded talking about quality but wanted to get equal time for the Heart Fund.

"We are going to make a company contribution; in fact, I have it right here, and we are willing to sign up for payroll deductions so that the employees can contribute in that manner."

She handed me an envelope containing a check. I put it in my pocket and thanked her for the contribution. She nodded, and we both rose to move to the conference room, where a small buffet was arranged. Most of the staff had already arrived, and I had the opportunity to meet each of them while we made ourselves sandwiches and conducted small talk.

After everyone was seated, the general manager (GM) made a little speech about the purpose of the session and stated that I had agreed to make some comments and then answer any questions anyone might have. Everyone was very polite and smiled at me. I had already eaten as much as I could quickly. Having attended hundreds of such luncheons in the course of my career, I knew that I would not get to pay much attention to my food. Watch the guest speaker at the next meal you attend and see if politeness doesn't suffer in order to assure that energy is provided.

I thanked them for inviting me, thanked them for the company contribution to the Heart Association, told them a little about the research activities that were going on, and offered a little hope that the disease might be better handled in the future as we knew more about it.

"There is a great parallel between preventing heart disease and running a successful company. We already know enough to reduce the incidence of heart disease dramatically. When individuals learn to manage weight, smoking, blood pressure, blood chemistry, stress, and such, they can significantly reduce the possibility of heart attack or stroke. The whole approach of 'wellness' for the person is wrapped around prevention.

"The same is true in companies. Most problems can be prevented from ever occurring. In fact, very few new problems do happen. Most of those we deal with every day are old friends; we learn how to solve them but don't do much about preventing them. Just as the procedure for heart bypass surgery can partially make up for years of eating the wrong things, so a company management can postpone the inevitable through the use of waivers and deviations.

"Customers are not as forgiving as our bodies are. They want things as promised and are not interested in excuses. Our bodies will let us adjust and compromise at least for a while. But eventually they, like customers, get tired of being treated poorly and bring the relationship to an end.

"Organizations don't have quality for only one reason: the management is not serious about it. They have not assigned it as the most important aspect of the business. Like the overweight, cigarette-smoking, nonexercising individual, they talk a good game, and plan a good strategy, but never get around to doing anything about it.

"Just as we have to deal with the whole body, so we have to deal with the whole company. We have to aim the operation at the customer, and we have to have clear instructions about what it takes to satisfy the customer. Then we have to manage the company in order to meet all those obligations. Management has to insist on that happening and set an example that others can follow.

"When all this is done, everyone will have pride in the company: the employees, the management, and the customers. Now I would be glad to chat about whatever anyone wants to chat about."

I looked around the room expectantly, but people were glancing at the ceiling, their fingernails, the empty sandwich plates. Finally one fellow raised his hand and said, somewhat angrily I thought: "I didn't understand a word you said."

"I'm sorry to hear that," I replied. "I was just trying to say that success is rather predictable. What you put in is what you get out."

"But we don't even try to do that around here. Why don't you tell us what you think about our company. Are we going to have a heart attack?"

Several of the others were frowning at him, but since this was the first sign of real life I had seen, I was delighted to continue the conversation.

"I think you have a point here. Why don't you tell me what is on your mind?"

He apparently had been thinking about all this for some time because he shook his head and moved right along.

"We have a customer who is about to leave us for another firm. They have been with us for some time, so I went to see them and asked what the problem was. They said that they just weren't getting good service from us, that every day a new person was dealing with them, that the stuff we sent them always had errors, that we didn't seem to care, and that we were just too much trouble."

The GM twisted in her seat and asked him to be more specific. What kind of errors did they find?

"Mostly procedural. We just didn't do a good job of finishing the presentation. We had to send a crew over there and do it in their operation."

"Was that Smith and Company?" asked one of the managers. When the speaker nodded, he continued.

"I know what happened there. We knew that wasn't going to be all done on time, but the people at Smith insisted on getting it, right or wrong. Now they come back and blame us. You remember I asked several of you if we should deliver it anyway and you all agreed."

"That is what I am talking about," said the first speaker. "If we were serious about customer satisfaction, we would never have delivered it. In fact, we would not have gotten this far at all. The problems wouldn't even exist if we thought about prevention."

"But that is unrealistic," said another. "I'm in charge of getting that work out, and I just can't cross every little 't' and dot every little 'i' and still meet schedule. We don't have enough people as it is. We need to be realistic above everything else."

The GM was pale. This was a little more than she had expected.

"What would you do," she asked me, "if customers said they wanted it anyway?"

"I would never send something to a customer that was not what we had promised to send. It might be necessary to go over there, apologize for the problem, tell them what was being done to prevent it in the future, and let them know when it would be delivered for sure. But as long as things can go out without being right, no one will believe you are serious about it."

"Would you mind telling us your impressions of our operation?" asked the GM.

"I usually don't do that," I replied. "However, I will make a couple of comments, and then I will send you all a copy of a grid I developed some years ago. You can evaluate yourself.

"As to comments, I would say that as a management team you seem to have good intentions, but you are not concentrating on the two most important parts of the business: the employees and the customers. You treat them both like abstracts. That is the same problem people have with preventing heart disease. They see no relationship between life habits and health.

"They eat whatever they want, exercise or don't depending on how they feel at the moment, and then wonder why things seem to go wrong. Here in this company there are obvious signs that the relationship between management and employees has not resulted in a great deal of pride. That is almost always caused by lack of consistency and attention.

"I wouldn't dream of being an instant expert on your company, but I would suggest you might begin with housekeeping. People do not take pride in a sloppy work area. And that habit extends over to dealing with customers.

"Also informality in dress and protocol is a positive thing in many situations, but it can easily extend into lack of respect for each other and the customer. Managers set the code by the way they behave and by the condition of their offices and attire. The company is a reflection of the attitudes of the people in this room."

Looking around I could see that they were a little startled. I have been telling clients the plain unvarnished truth for so long that I forgot these people weren't clients.

"Do you want the contribution back?" I asked.

They all laughed good naturedly, and we broke up.

About a year later I ran into the general manager in the mall. She waved me over to where she was standing with two of her children, who immediately proved my theory that kids can spot a grandfather anywhere. It becomes a sort of take-off of the song from *Finnian's Rainbow:* "When I'm not near the grandfather I love, I love the one I'm near." In between my listening to the latest happenings in grade school, she asked me if I could possibly drop by their operation again.

"It is time for the Heart Fund contribution, and the staff wanted to present it to you personally. They appreciated your taking such an interest in them."

There was no way I could pass that up, so about 10 days later I appeared in the lobby. The place had been redecorated, and the receptionist had a uniform. The office area was neat, no messy desks, the people were dressed in business attire, no one was wandering around, and the walls were brightly painted. It was a dramatic change.

"We practically had to call in the Board of Health to get this place cleaned up," said my hostess as she led me into her immaculate office. "But once we got started, everyone became absolutely enthusiastic. Now we bring customers, and potential ones, in for meetings here. They are very impressed and in a positive way."

"We have regular meetings with the employees to discuss problems and opportunities and, frankly, we all are becoming proud of the company and our work. We appreciate your being honest with us."

We had a nice little lunch in the conference room again, and they presented another check for the Heart Association. They had raised their donation by an amount equal to my daily consulting fee (having checked that out with my secretary). They also indicated that the entire corporation was considering coming to our firm for assistance since the managers saw the improvement here. I noticed that they did not ask my opinion of their current management style, but I complimented them on their progress anyway. We now have an ongoing and more formal relationship. They have gotten closer to reality and are quite successful.

This is a case of a management that got off the track and blamed everyone but itself. Once the managers' attention returned to the employees and customers, they were able to grow and prosper in business. As long as they were sitting around complaining about things instead of working hard with those employees and customers, the company slowly drifted into sloppy habits. The tacky environment produced tacky thinking, and everything really did get worse. But when an outsider took one look and sniffed that they certainly weren't very good housekeepers, they revolted and went into a "we'll show him" attack. As the management began to show some signs of life, the people did all the things they knew should have been done anyway. It happens every time.

Pride brings out the best in people; arrogance brings out the worst. A golfer awarded a Master's jacket would never consider dishonoring that piece of cloth under any circumstances. A member of a street gang is proud of the jacket earned by some act of violence. The tradition behind the memento is the important factor. Traditions can be established for good or evil. Sometimes the result is contrary to the intent.

Unions were first formed for the purpose of bringing together those who had no rights or protection. By presenting management with a choice of dealing with the workers' organization or going out of business, they won the day. The members were proud of the union, and the union was the members. During my boyhood in West Virginia, the miners' union and the steelworkers' union fought for basic rights. Workers died for decent treatment. Without the unions this would not be a nation of pride. I lived through all that and will forever respect what had to happen. Knowing people on both sides of the fence, and knowing that they were decent, caring individuals, it was hard to believe that so much suffering had to occur to change things. But there apparently was no other way to overcome such misconceptions.

Over the years many labor organizations became so concerned with political power, with intimidating management, and with continual increases in wages and benefits that they lost touch with reality. Membership became something that had to be rather than something that was done through pride. As a result, union membership is on the decrease, union influence is declining, and workers are in danger of being oppressed again, although in a different manner from before.

We have seen in the restructuring of basic industry in America that many jobs have been lost in order to restate the companies into a form that would let them compete worldwide. In the process many powerful unions have been shown to be ineffective at protecting their members. Faced with cooperate-or-die decisions, they have gone along with the companies. They could have helped meet the challenge if they had been more willing to become involved with management on a closer basis. Perhaps many jobs could have been saved. But many labor leaders lost sight of the purpose of the unions. It could have been different, and in some cases it was.

In the machine tool industry, for instance, computers were developed to run the machines that create tools. What could be done to save the toolmakers? Cooperation between union leadership and management produced a solution that would not have been considered before: managers taught the toolmakers to run computers. Valuable skills were saved; apprenticeship programs continue. It is a good solution that didn't happen in the newspaper printing business because of stubborness and the wrong type of pride.

But even though the blue collar jobs have dropped off in the basic industries, the white collar ones have grown in number. So, in fact, there are more jobs available, which isn't much consolation if you are a diehard steel mill worker.

But now management is beginning to re-create, in the knowledge areas, what previous generations of leaders established in the broader field of labor. Managers are treating these workers with disrespect and inattention. It won't be long before white collar unions will become necessary. The largest union in the nation at present is the teachers. They learned that it was not possible for an individual teacher to deal successfully with school boards and professional administrators.

So when companies decide to lay off 15 percent of the staff in order to meet short-term cost pressures and they treat people poorly in the process, they are sowing seeds of another 1934. That makes for conflict, which cuts pride out of the relationship for a generation at least. People will just not give their all to an organization that won't give them proper consideration.

The basics of creating pride are

- The organization has to have clear goals and objectives that the employees can respect.

- The management has to be consistently dedicated to having everyone understand and be able to meet the performance requirements that will cause the organization to reach those goals and objectives.

- There must be continuous education and communication that lets the employees know what is happening and forces management to listen to both employees and customers.

- There must be an awareness, positively reinforced, that shows this is an organization worthy of pride.

- Any downturn or unfortunate incident must be faced openly and directly.

  In short: "Do unto others as you would have others do unto you."

PART 2
The Masters Corporation Case

8

A Shocking Discovery

My name is George Kales. I am chairperson and CEO of Masters Corporation. I thought that a description of the events we have gone through here at Masters could be useful to others who might face similar situations. Managing today is nothing like it was when I started a dozen years ago. Today the half-life of a CEO is about one year. Not too many years ago it was possible to set the firm on cruise control and just watch for traffic jams or railroad crossings. It is all different now; eternal vigilance is now the price of success.

Competitors and cost control used to be what kept CEOs awake nights. Now takeover artists and the necessity for ever improving quarterly results, plus life in a world economy, have added to the toll. What used to be wonderful management skills are now just routine. It is necessary to prepare for the future continually and not only prepare for the future but prepare to prevent problems. Staying out of the quicksand is much better than getting a good deal on a towing contract.

I have been involved here for 12 years, and in that time we built this company into a worldwide operation of insurance and manufacturing. At the time my story begins, we had built a strong management team and had low debt and a steadily building business. In short, everything was going well by all the normal standards of performance. The analysts loved us; we were selling at a good multiple. The cash flow was positive, and the people seemed to be happy.

Our Board is strong and sufficiently independent to have made it clear some time ago that I needed to prepare a succession pattern. I have done that to their satisfaction and mine. I have stepped back from the day-to-day operations and have concentrated on overall strategy and building a younger management team. It has worked out very well so far, but I am still spending most of my time thinking of how the corporation could be shaped so that it would continue to be a growing prosperous place, perhaps forever.

Masters is a corporation with $540 million in revenue and $32,400,000 income. The Insurance Division produces $12,960,000 of the income; Manufacturing provides the remainder. No one is happy with this return. There are 4000 employees in Manufacturing and 1445 in Insurance. Masters used to have an annual growth rate of at least 20 percent and a return after tax of 10 percent or better. In the past three years both have slipped, for many reasons.

At my suggestion the president asked the managers of these two divisions to evaluate themselves according to the ESO profile. Now that isn't really going to do a lot of good all by itself. They think they are wonderful, and I'm sure any evaluation they conduct will reveal that. This is the problem with self-help things, very little actual help can be accomplished unless the individual or organization is prepared to admit that it is required. The attitude begins at age two and hardens as life goes on.

Human beings in general don't naturally lean to asking for assistance on personal inadequacies. Almost everyone has some failing or problem that could be improved if he or she only recognizes that it exists. My parents drank a great deal more than they needed to but refused to even consider that it was causing problems. They grew to believe that the world was out of line and became very negative about it all. It was a shame because they were really warm, loving people. Drugs will do that too.

Success is a kind of drug in the business world. It doesn't take long before the people running a place become convinced that it is their own personality and personal charm that causes everything to hum in unison. Vic Hakel in Insurance appears to be developing that thought pattern. The fact that the insurance investments are doing well has little to do with it in his mind. Investment is where the profit comes from in the insurance business, as we know. Management's job is to keep the premiums coming in, the expenses down, and the investments producing.

Pearl Turner in Manufacturing doesn't have as many illusions because she worked her way up through the shops after coming out of MBA school. She knows how hard it is to make a buck in those areas. But some of her staff think it will go on forever. In both cases the marketing plans are not the least bit people-sensitive; even Human Resources doesn't seem interested in the troops.

Ever since I suggested to the Board that it make Phil Moore the president of Masters, he has been trying to move our management teams toward a longer-range management style. He has a clear vision of how vital that style is. We have been talking about the actions necessary to give this corporation the opportunity to be eternally successful.

The other day I wandered into Phil's office while he was working at his blackboard, which really is white and is marked on with a felt-tipped pen. There are some things I will never quite get comfortable with, and "white board" is one of them. Phil seems to bustle continuously, regardless of what task is underway, which makes a good contrast to my pattern which has been described more than once as "lumbering."

He turned and smiled as I walked in and then came over to shake my hand and offer a seat. It is amazing how many executives do not take the time to perform these little courtesies. People who see to your every need when you visit their home act like tax collectors in their office. I believe that the occupant of an office should get up when anyone comes in and see to the guest before conducting business. Even if the individual has been invited there to be chewed out, he or she should be treated like a person.

"I'm glad you dropped by, George," said Phil. "I have been trying to get some thoughts together for this corporate wellness conference we are going to have."

"'Wellness?' I hadn't thought to call it that."

"Well it makes corporate strategy into something people can relate to. Everyone is into personal wellness, I just want to apply the same concept of keeping well to corporations."

He waved his pen at me and moved back to the writing area. Phil was raised in the marketing field, and perhaps because of that, almost automatically put things into analogies with the hope they would be easier to understand. And I think he was on the mark with this one, corporate wellness was really what we were trying to cause.

"I have been working on this from two angles. First we need to get people interested in the thought of never having to conduct an improvement program because they never let things get away from them. If you don't gain 25 extra pounds, you don't have to sweat and strain to get rid of it."

He nodded expectantly to see if I grasped all this. Obediently I nodded back to signal that I did indeed and that it was making sense up to this point. He took off his coat jacket, laid it across the chair, and moved over to a flip chart. Turning the cover, he revealed the page on which had been written:

- Concern—family organizations
- Loyalty—college organizations
- Efficiency—public organizations

"I remember that," I said. "It is what an author laid out as the best characteristics of the different organizations. He believed that if you could combine them, then everything had a better chance of lasting forever."

"Right," he replied. "And if we dig a little deeper we can see that the 'concern' applies primarily to the people, the 'loyalty' to the institution itself, and the 'efficiency' to management skills. All those can be identified, measured, and caused.

"The problem is that it all appears to be quite obvious, which is usually true of good ideas. That is why they are hard to sell. So I am trying to work it around to something that will sell itself."

He sat down and looked expectantly at me. This is why most corporate Boards try to have a chairperson who is older and more experienced than the president. It gives the president someone to look expectantly at. Unfortunately, he was getting ahead of me, so all I could do was comment encouragingly.

"Perhaps we could make it harder to understand. At any rate, who do you want to sell it to?"

"To our management team. Like you keep telling me, we can't get executives to really become involved in something unless they feel ownership. This will let them have something they can grab onto and at the same time provide tracks to keep the corporation on. If we can really learn how to use the Systems Integrity Function, we will be able to keep the beast on those tracks.

"We spend so much time on numbers and projections that we can lose sight of what the company is doing and not doing. No matter how hard we try to ignore the demands of quarterly performance, we are bound to it. We have to have a long-range concept for managing that is ground inside the minds of our leaders."

He was back on his feet again and turning to a new page. Just as he was about to begin laying out his plan for the conference, my assistant came in with a reminder that I was supposed to have an Audit Committee lunch. Three of the outside Board directors and the Systems Integrity director were about to arrive.

"I will have to get back with you, Phil," I said. "It looks to me like we're on the right path. The sooner we bring the executive team in on this, the better off we'll be. We don't want to give them the impression that we are trying to manipulate them, of course."

Phil moved around to the front of the desk and sat back against it.

"I agree that we don't want to manipulate them; it wouldn't work anyway; they are too smart for that. But I think that we can make certain they understand how seriously we need to learn how to practice management in order to secure the future for this organization. I don't want them to treat this like it is just another status review. What do you suggest I do at this point to not get accused of Machiavellian tendencies?"

I shrugged my shoulders. Part of my plan was to get away from giving a lot of direction, and Phil was not one who needed much anyway. But this was probably a proper time for a little advice, if not guidance.

"You might think about bringing Victor and Pearl into the planning sessions. Then they will be able to make sure it gets the proper consideration from their folks."

"I had planned to do that later, but it is probably a good idea to bring them in now. I'll take care of that this afternoon. On another subject, what would you think about doing a follow up at the senior management conference? All the marketing people together, and the purchasing and such? Of course, they meet anyway as part of their regular life...."

I "lumbered" off toward the door.

"Up to you, Philip, up to you. I think if we can get people to understand the basics, they will take care of the implementation. See you at the Finance meeting; don't forget that they are going to discuss the new computer system."

I went out to the hall and pushed the elevator button. If I could have my way, we would have only one-story buildings, all the walls would be glass, and everyone could see each other all the time. There is no communication in a large building.

The Audit Committee used to be a rather dry affair. We would invite the managing partner of the auditing company to come in and give us a lecture, wonder if anyone is stealing from the company, and have lunch. However, recently the outside directors who, with myself, make up the membership of the committee, have become interested in what is happening in other than the traditional areas of audit. So they asked for current status from the Systems Integrity Department and have learned a great deal about the corporation's workings. This has been a good news, bad news activity to me. They ask a lot of questions on subjects they didn't even worry about before. It makes a little more work for the staff, but the end result has been positive since the directors, as well as the staff, know more about the operations now and are quite helpful.

As I was walking down to the conference room, I caught up with Roger Alston, the custodian, who was balancing two boxes containing the Audit Committee lunch. I rushed ahead to open the door for him and helped set the boxes on the table.

"Thank you Mr. Kales," he said. "I always think I am going to be able to carry boxes and open doors, too, but it always works out the same way. It just can't be done the way we are designed. I have been working on a mechanical arm that I could strap to my back and call it out to turn knobs."

He was earnestly distributing the deli lunch and drinks around the side table as he talked. Roger had been with Masters since before I came and, as far as I know, had never missed a day of work.

"Roger, if you can get that perfected, we will be glad to produce it for you. I'll bet we could sell a million a year," I said.

He nodded.

"Well the last 50 inventions I had didn't ever get produced, but I'll keep you in mind if this one works out." He smiled again and left me alone.

I have no problem remembering when white tablecloth executive dining rooms were quite routine in our size company. In the past we would be having this Board committee in a private room with oak furniture, wine, and discreetly served meals. But the advantages of privacy and style were far overcome by the impression such rooms left with those who did not get to use them.

We have eliminated all separate dining in every facility throughout the corporation. Everyone eats in the employee's dining area, and they serve excellent food. For a really private meeting, held at lunch in order to conserve time, we send down to the deli across the street and order material to make sandwiches. It works out very well, and no one falls asleep after a heavy lunch.

I first became aware that secluded dining was causing a problem when I visited one of our midwest offices and discovered in conversation that one of the biggest personnel problems was determining who should have dining room privileges. The human resources director was telling me about the impatience of youth. Some of the younger people were objecting to not being eligible for the perk, and a couple had actually quit. Since we had spent a good deal of money and energy developing them up to that point, it seemed silly to lose them over such an item. We had created the situation ourselves.

"They really attached a lot of significance to being members of the executive dining room," he said. "I explained that there was only so much room, but it made no difference. I am recommending that we set up a sort of junior room for those folks. Then they will feel properly recognized until they reach the level that they can join the executive dining room. We'll have a procedure out on it in a month or so. I'll make certain you get to see it; it might serve as a guide for other sites."

At that moment I decided that this was one perk that had outlived its usefulness. The original idea was to give senior executives the routine opportunity to spend time together while doing something they had to do anyway—eat lunch. Over the years it had become a sort of informal club denoting privilege. Instead of a place of convenience and communication, it had become a source of controversy and disruption.

I shook my head.

"I think we are going to have to recognize that the executive dining room is no longer good for the company. How about making that procedure one on how we get rid of them throughout the corporation?"

He looked at me with what I can only interpret as an amused expression. Then he actually smiled.

"That would be wonderful," he said. "I have been wanting to get rid of them for some time. But frankly, George, the feeling has been that you thought they were important. They will be gone, and the space will be used for something more useful in a few weeks. I am really glad you made that decision. The Human Resources directors will probably elect you person of the year."

Later I began to wonder how many other obsolete things we were doing because "the feeling has been that" I wanted it that way. I decided that management was going to have to work harder to make itself clear, on everything.

My daydreaming came to an abrupt halt when Al Watts came into the room. Al had been a board member for 20 years. He was the semiretired chairperson of a steel company.

"How are you George?" he smiled as he pounded me on the shoulder.

"You look like you were plotting against the world, or at least the Audit Committee. Don't be so serious about all this stuff. This company is so controlled there couldn't be anything for an audit to find, except that we spend a fortune auditing so no one can steal from us.

"The probability of a company this size having an embezzler is about 40 percent, according to my guess. The probability of having two of them is about 5 percent. Three would be zero. So what we ought to do is employ someone to do a little modest stealing, and then the odds would be such that we wouldn't have to hire all these audit firms and do all that internal checking."

"It's no wonder they don't let you serve on the golf handicap committee," said Vincent de Bray, entering the room. As he shook our hands and placed his briefcase at the table, Vincent quickly assessed the luncheon layout and began to assemble a sandwich. He was never one to waste any time.

"I've got some ideas about handicaps too, Vincent," nodded Al. "But I wouldn't want to interfere with your side income. I hear that the people at your club pay protection to keep from falling in your clutches."

"The finance business isn't what it used to be; a fellow has to pick up what he can where he can. Is Foster coming?"

"As far as I know," I said. "I talked to him last week about putting some of our insurance people into his stores, and he said he would be here."

"Is that a good idea?" asked Al. "I would think that the independent agents would be upset with our going in competition with them."

"Actually it would be their people, Al. We would just provide the framework and then sort of franchise it to the independents. The retail stores want to deal with us as the parent company."

"That sounds like the beginning of banking in the mall," said Vincent. "Perhaps our firm could work out something if there is room for two in the booth. Who is running all this for you, Eleanor Landry?"

"She's the one. I'm sure she would be glad to talk to your folks about doing something together," I replied.

Al shook his head.

"You wheeler-dealers always think about positioning products, but you forget people. No one is going to be able to shop for insurance or a loan with two kids hanging on them, and their neighbors walking past. Malls are for advertising, explaining, and getting them interested. Then invite them to the office."

I pulled out a chair and laid my paper plate on the table in front of it. I really enjoyed these people; they had so much experience that even casual conversation was stimulating. However, they were not the kind who quote "It has to be that way" proverbs all the time. They were open to new thoughts and then tested them against their formidable experience bank.

Just as I was about to say we should begin without Foster, he came in followed by the Systems Integrity Director,

Cynthia Elliott. "I wanted to get in here before Cynthia," said Foster. "She would probably turn me in for being late. But it wasn't my fault, I was delayed by a broker asking me what the company's stock was going to do."

Cynthia smiled.

"I hope you'll let us know as soon as you figure it out."

Foster grimaced.

"I have been around Wall Street all my working life, and I don't know any more about what is going to happen now than the day I came here. My grandmother kept her money in a 4 percent savings and loan account and she has made more than I have with all my hanging out with the financial world."

Al punched Foster in the side and headed him to the buffet.

"Whenever I hear some retailers talking about how they never made any money, I know it is time to lock up my assets. You can get more out of nothing than anyone I ever saw. How do you keep expenses down so close and still serve the customers and keep the people happy at the same time? What's your secret?"

Foster grinned at the backhanded compliment. He was proud of his reputation as a cost-conscious executive. It had paid off for his department stores. They were still thriving and growing in spite of all the discount operations that were around.

"Retailing is the real world," he said. "We have to identify our fixed costs like properties and personnel, then control the inventory precisely, price the merchandise so it will have a continuous flow out, and pick the right stuff to sell so there is no flow back in.

"Ours is a nickel here, dime there business. We sell items that range from a few cents to thousands of dollars, but each has to make its contribution; we can't go on averages like you people do. I would be willing to wager the cost of this gourmet lunch that none of you knows what it costs to open your doors each morning. You make budgets and deal with the costs after the fact. We can't do that in retailing.

"Some people look at a store and see counters full of merchandise. I look at those same counters and see trays full of dollar bills, my dollar bills. The idea is to exchange mine for the customer's."

He went over to the table, picked up a piece of pecan pie and began to eat it while standing there.

"Banking is a different kind of business, Foster," said Vincent. "We deal in intangibles. But I will say that we do not monitor our expenses the way you do; we are somewhat sloppy on that."

"It is easy to be sloppy when you pay out 5 percent for money and get back 14 percent for the same stuff," commented Al. "And you don't even have to package it. I have to grind my raw material, melt it, pour it, roll it, cool it, package it, deliver it, and then listen to the complaints. And we are lucky if we make 2 percent after tax. I'll be glad to trade businesses with you any time."

I rapped the table and motioned for everyone to take a seat.

"I would like to continue this management seminar, but right now we have to get on with the business of the Masters Corporation. This is the Audit Committee of the Board and I call it to order now, noting that we have a quorum. The corporate secretary has entrusted me with the task of taking the minutes of the meeting."

"We have handled all the formal business of the year at this time, having selected the auditing firm and accepted the internal auditor's report on the inventory audit. The only agenda item we have today is the Systems Integrity Department's report that we requested several months ago. Cynthia has come by today to discuss it with us. Cynthia, thank you for coming. Please go ahead with your report."

I sat back as she walked around to the front of the table and handed each of us a folder containing the report. She had really brought this evaluation business to a professional level. The executives trusted her results and appreciated her personal discretion.

"We were asked to do an opinion survey of Masters based on the 'Eternally Successful Organization' format of five characteristics. The Insurance and Manufacturing groups are doing the same thing for themselves. We should be able to compare those reports with this one at future Audit Committee meetings.

"The report I have handed you is somewhat detailed, although I remind you that it is opinion-based and should not be considered a scientific study. On the first page I have put together a summary of the findings. Perhaps it would be useful if we covered them before getting into the details."

She paused and look around the table. Everyone was flipping through the report while nodding in agreement.

"Let me ask, Cynthia," said Al, "Do you know of any other company doing such a report?"

"I don't know of any published ones, Mr. Watts," she replied, "but I do know that many are considering looking at themselves this way. They don't seem to know exactly what to do about it all yet. Most of the deficiencies that are found require complicated and deep changes in the way the business is run."

"That is usually true with any new way of looking at things," commented Vincent. "I remember the first time someone brought up the subject of computerizing the back rooms of the banks. We had no idea how backward we were, and even when we found out, it was very difficult to get the resources to fix it."

"If I remember right," said Foster, "it was necessary to place several very senior people onto a recognition plaque in the lobby in order to get it done."

"We put several on one plaque. But it did take a real change in management thinking. The stock market went through that same thing. If it hadn't automated, it would now be extinct. Can you imagine handling 400-million-share days with ballpoint pens?"

Cynthia was waiting while all this went on, looking for an opening. When the comments had run their course, she asked us to turn to page 1 and began.

"The first characteristic is: 'People do things right routinely.'

"We gave the corporation a Progressive Care rating on this

one. Most of the organization is entering a quality improvement process under the guidance of a consulting firm. Also, we know that many executives worry about quality. So we gave it a Progressive Care for effort. As soon as they get really involved, we will take another look," she said.

I was really concerned about this one. I thought we were doing well with quality. We certainly have spent enough on it.

"Let's look at the whole picture before we get off on one item. Are we that bad all over?"

"You can see the evaluation," said Cynthia. "It doesn't look all that wonderful, and don't forget it was done by people who work here. I figure they have been kind."

People do things right routinely.	= Progressive Care
Growth is profitable and steady.	= Healing
Customer needs are the priority.	= Progressive Care
Change is planned and managed.	= Intensive Care
People are proud to work there.	= Progressive Care

Vincent shook his head.

"That isn't a very good report card, but I have to say that the bank probably would not have done that well. Our growth has been good, but the customer is a dim second in our thoughts and no one has hugged me lately to say what a wonderful place this is to work."

"I am going to have to do this in the stores, but I think it will be better to have a consultant handle it. I seriously doubt that we could get such an honest report," said Foster.

"The new mill would probably be all Healings," said Al. "The old mills would be Comotose, but Cynthia is much too polite to do that to us."

I was still in shock. I was assuming we were much better

managed than this. The divisions would certainly give themselves much better reports when they met to go over it with Phil. At least I think they would.

The room was quiet for a few moments. So I decided we needed to go to the next step.

"How about going over the highlights of each characteristic, Cynthia? I'd like to get a better feel for some of the specifics that determine the ratings."

"Okay," she said. "Remembering that these are unscientific ratings, although many of them are backed up by real data; let me point out some of the situations and indications that led us to this way of thinking."

"First, the 'not doing things right' is probably the clearest datum we have. Some of our people went off to the Quality College two years ago, but then we decided to do quality improvement inside and terminated that relationship. We have now reopened it because we found out that doing it ourselves was not a good idea. Our program was aimed at the bottom of the organization, and management never did get involved. We also learned that you can't teach executives from inside a company. They all have their own agendas."

"However, the accountants did learn how to calculate the Price of Nonconformance which tells us what it costs to do things wrong. In Manufacturing that includes warranty, rework, and such. There the cost amounted to 29.6 percent of sales, or $91 million. In Insurance it was figured as a percent of operating cost and came out at 33 percent, or around $52 million, but they think that is low."

I really was shocked.

"You are talking about $143 million. That is a figure I have never heard before. None of these numbers has been used in the operating meetings. Why is that?"

Cynthia shrugged.

"The Quality people felt that the costs needed more investigation and have been looking into it for the past 18 months. But we have checked them out, and the Accounting Department vouches for these numbers although the staff thinks more is involved."

"You don't need more to scare the daylights out of a person," said Al. "We made 12 percent pretax last year in Masters and spent three or four times that doing things wrong."

"Boy, this could be a marvelous opportunity," said Foster. "I've got to figure out how much that will be in a retail property. It has to be 40 percent. Cynthia I need the address of that Quality College."

I motioned to Cynthia to continue.

"Growth received a relatively good rating because we have been doing that internally and the few acquisitions we made were in the industry and filled in gaps. Also we do a good job of training new people so they don't foul things up while they are learning. The sales department is particularly well trained."

She seemed pleased with this part of the report. I had noticed that she was somewhat taken aback with the reaction of the three of us to the cost of quality report. She had recovered, but inside I was boiling. It was unbelievable that this information had not been openly brought out by the quality control people, as well as accounting, no matter how wonderful the reason.

"Third," she continued, "is the customer component. That was rated as Progressive Care and probably could be a little lower. The big problem here is that although we do a lot of customer contact and surveying, almost none of that gets to any of the operating areas. It is all held in Marketing and dribbled out according to the needs of the business."

Foster sat up; this was his area of interest. Retail stores let you see the customer face to face any time you wish to step out of the office and onto the floor. Other businesses were not that direct.

"Could that explain why we had to pull back that new casualty insurance program last year and redo the advertising approach? If I remember correctly, the decision was that the customers did not respond at all to our concept."

"That is correct," I replied. "We found out that people were not interested in plain old life insurance anymore. They wanted to tie in with estate management, real estate, and investments. We missed the boat entirely. But I hadn't known it because we didn't use the information we had."

"Fourth," said Cynthia, "is the management of change. There we received a unanimous agreement that the company does a terrible job in both causing and controlling change. It recognizes change and moves toward it well, but no one ever knows about it. Setting up Systems Integrity is beginning to help in this area, but management acceptance of SI has not been that terrific. Managers feel threatened."

"Threatened?" I blurted. "How could that be? We have explained Systems Integrity and how it is the executives' friend for months. How could they feel threatened?"

"It doesn't take much to threaten management," said Al. "We are a bunch of paranoids, and insecure at that. It makes you wonder. We all come equipped with beliefs and assumptions and anxieties. One time when I thought everything was going so well, and this was a long time ago, I invited all my staff to lunch on an impulse. I discovered later that they had all decided we were going to have a big reorganization and were nervous the whole lunch time. When it was all over, and nothing had happened, the consensus was that I had decided to wait for a while before announcing it."

I just didn't agree with the thought that they were refusing to cooperate.

"Let's stop here a moment, Cynthia. I'd like to call the comptroller in here so after we are finished with the overview, we can examine some of those Price of Nonconformance numbers."

I reached behind me for the telephone and then paused trying to remember the number.

"Sandy's number is 4290," said Cynthia. "I asked him to be available this morning in case you all wanted to hear more about the Price of Nonconformance."

I dialed the number and Sandy answered. He still had a trace of the Deep South in his voice even after all these years in the big city.

"Sandy, we are going over some information with Cynthia

and would like to know more about these Price of Nonconformance numbers. Are those real? Are we really throwing
away more than $100 million a year?"

"It sure looks like it George," he said. "We have been doing
an analysis on it. Would you like me to bring it over?"

"That's what I had in mind, Sandy. Come ahead when
you're ready. We are in the conference room and will even
buy you some lunch. See you in a little bit."

I turned to the others and motioned Cynthia to continue.

"The fifth characteristic is personal pride in working for
the company, and that was rated a C. The biggest concerns
here related to employees not feeling as if they are a part of
the organization and wondering about the future of the company. The rating was much better before the Insurance Division shut down its data network and laid off all those
people."

"But most of those who were laid off went to work for the
new operation," I whined. This was not turning out to be a
fun morning at all.

"They don't know that, George," said Cynthia. "Most of
our problem seems to come from not having formal communication systems within the company. We don't even have a
company newspaper any more."

Foster thought about this comment and then remarked
that he remembered neither division wanted to put the paper
on its budget back when we divided the corporation into
Manufacturing and Insurance. As a result it was set aside.

"A paper would help, but it takes a lot of people-to-people
contact to keep the family atmosphere going," commented
Vincent. "Once a company gets past a hundred people, communication has to be forced. That is also part of the change
control problem. Some folks just don't read or even notice
what is going on. Getting everyone on the same frequency
takes a lot of work, but it has to be done."

"We have only six in our family, and it is a full-time effort
just to figure out where they all are at any given moment;
forget knowing what is going on," said Al.

I was looking toward the door every few moments, waiting

for Sandy. This evaluation was beginning to come together in my head. We were going to have a lot of work to do and a wonderful opportunity to change this company for the better. All I had to do was get it back to a business thing in my mind and quit taking it personally.

Taking things into myself has always been a problem for me. I would take offense at the way someone had acted or become upset with what I thought was a stupid decision, and it would keep me awake. The only cure was to face the person and find out what really happened (it never was as bad as I had thought) or write a scathing memo in the middle of the night that I knew would never be mailed. That would let me go to sleep.

Sandy's arrival disrupted my daydream, and as we got him seated I was thinking about what we really needed to learn at this meeting.

"Can you give us the highlights of where this money goes? And I would also like to understand how come it isn't reported this way routinely. Can we do that?"

"Sure," he said. "Let me begin with the second part. When it is reported, all these numbers are included in one account number or another. Rework, for instance, which accounts for a good bit of Manufacturing's expense, is listed as a line item. We haven't pulled all these that are identified as 'Price of Nonconformance' together before. It is done as a procedural item rather than part of the accounting system in the computer. We can start doing that if you would like."

"I would like," I said.

"So the $141 million is in the overall numbers of the company but not pulled out as waste. It would be something like automobile expense, which could be in several accounts but never recognized as a whole," said Foster.

"Yes, and that is the normal way of doing it. The problem with it, of course, is that categories don't really get looked at. Frankly, I had never heard of the Price of Nonconformance before a few months ago, but it is really a powerful tool. Let me show you where the money goes. I have a view graph. Perhaps I could show it on the machine."

"I'll get the screen and lights," volunteered Cynthia.

"You modern businesswomen won't let anyone do anything for you," said Al.

"Don't get any wrong ideas," said Cynthia. "I stand in front of doors for hours waiting for someone to come along and open them for me. In this case I am just anxious to see the breakout."

Sandy mounted the chart and turned on the machine. "The numbers have been rounded off to make them easier to read," said Sandy. "Here we are talking about Price of Nonconformance for the Manufacturing Division."

PRICE OF NONCONFORMANCE: Manufacturing Division

Item	Cost
Rework	$19,000,000
Warranty and field service	23,000,000
Excess inventory	20,000,000
Scrap	10,000,000
Excess overtime	2,000,000
Appraisal	17,000,000
	$91,000,000

Not included: Lost sales due to quality, $22,000,000.

PRICE OF NONCONFORMANCE (Prevention): Manufacturing Divison

Item	Cost
Education and training	$ 250,000
Product qualification	600,000
Systems integrity	475,000
	$1,325,000

There was a long period of silence as we studied the numbers. Then Foster spoke.

"So we spend $91 million doing things wrong and $1.3 million preventing spending the $91 million? That seems backward. What would a proper education program cost us?"

"It depends, of course, on what you want to teach and to how many. But I do know that the quality education and implementation that we decided not to do a year or so ago would have cost us around $125 per employee starting with the Board and working down. About three days of the PONC [Price of Nonconformance] expense," said Cynthia.

"It was thought that we could do the same thing inside," said Sandy. "So Personnel and Quality set up some courses, mostly on statistics and problem solving, but I think they didn't do anything for management, which is where the main causes lie."

"It must not have had much effect on anyone," I noted. "What do the Insurance numbers look like? They don't have scrap or warranty; where do they find to dump 52 million bucks?"

"You'd be surprised," said Sandra. "From what I have learned, and then checked out in my own areas, white collar workers are about 50 percent effective. Half the people are off chasing something old or fixing something new. Believe me, George, this whole thing is scary. No one looks at performance in this way."

PRICE OF NONCONFORMANCE: Insurance Division

Item	Cost
Reprocessing	$24,000,000
Field service	7,000,000
Receivables overdue interest	2,000,000
Agent hot line	2,000,000
State tax double payment	1,000,000
Computer debugging down-time	5,000,000
Appraisal	11,000,000
	$52,000,000

Not included: Sales personnel turnover, $9,000,000.

PRICE OF CONFORMANCE: Insurance Division

Item	Cost
Quality education and training	$ 37,000
Systems integrity	250,000
	$287,000

Foster nodded in approval. "I like to see things spelled out like this. I'm going to do the same thing in our stores. We'll get consultants to help us out. But a lot of these costs have to come from lack of change control, people not having pride in the organization, customer data not being utilized, and such. Every company I have ever known has these same problems. But you folks are looking at them and doing something about it, or plan to do something about it. That is good."

I could see that the other directors felt the same way. They were very grown up, so I should have recognized that they would view this as a challenge, not as an impending disaster.

I decided it was time to close the meeting. "If we can solve these problems and learn how to prevent them from occurring in the future, we will be on our way to being eternally successful. Phil already has some things going that this will fit into, and I will forcefully encourage that, and more, coming about."

"I suggest that this committee keep track of what progress is being made so we can advise the Board on the subject. I will make sure you receive the minutes of team and strategy meetings."

"This has been the best meeting I have ever attended, George," said Al. "I mean that. This is a whole new way of looking at a corporation, a people-oriented way. A lot of things need to be done. Good luck."

We adjourned and planned to reconvene next month. I asked Cynthia to schedule the division presidents to come and share their status with us on the ESO rating. At Vincent's suggestion we will do one each month. That will give us time to absorb the data.

In the meantime, I am going back to study the CEO business, I think my half-life is getting closer to quarter life.

9
Probing for a Plan

I had left what I have come to call the "ESO Session" with a real concern. It seemed to me that the company was falling apart, regardless of all the brave and challenging words that were spoken. I began to realize later that we had never looked at Masters in that fashion before, so it may have been unfair to react so strongly. But I stayed irritated anyway and headed right for Phil Moore's office.

He was just putting his charts away and getting ready to go to the airport. I didn't waste time on preliminaries.

"Have you seen that Price of Nonconformance report that says we are wasting $143 million every year? We were just looking at it in the Audit Committee, and I am very concerned."

Phil smiled and nodded and encouraged me to sit down and relax. He went to his desk and picked a folder out of several that were piled to the right of his blotter pad.

"It just came to my attention, and I am concerned also. I was having copies made so we can include it in the material to be discussed at the strategy session with the presidents. Cynthia sent me the ESO evaluation, too, and I have to say that it shook me up. We really have to get hold of this situation."

I was pleased that he was not being defensive about this.

We needed to take positive action and didn't have time to fool around.

"Good, I'm glad you found that report interesting. It shows we have a lot of room to improve. We are going to have to put a team together to absorb all this and determine what actions to take. But it involves every part of the company."

He sat across from me.

"Let me get the strategy sessions over with. I think the executives will come to the same conclusion. Then it will be easier to work it all to the company's advantage. But correction is going to require skills, knowledge, and materials that we don't have. How do you feel about using consultants?"

This is a subject that had always concerned me. Obviously we couldn't fix our own teeth, or take out our own appendix, or, in my case anyway, even do my own tax return. For those jobs, specialists were required. But, having done the job, they should disappear, having prepared us to handle it in the future.

"There are consultants and consultants. I don't want a bunch of people who disrupt operations and stick around forever. We need a firm, or firms, with an intensive, internally conducted training program for its people; originally developed generic material; the ability to create tailored things just for us, if we need them; and the ability to teach us to teach what we learn from them so we can keep up-to-date forever. The firm should have a reputation for integrity and effectiveness, and we would expect it to be financially secure so we know it will be around for some time. What it costs is important but should not be a selection criterion because what the right firm is going to save us will be many times what it costs. You and I will help pick the firm. Don't let Purchasing do it; they are only price-oriented."

Phil nodded in agreement.

"My experience has been that companies make the contact points with consultants too low in the organization. We'll keep it with the executive team that is in charge of overcoming."

"We are already getting help in Quality—to get us on an overall quality management program. We will need assistance in Human Resources—to help with the Pride issue—and Communications—probably a public relations firm or such. That will be some handful to deal with but will give us the staff assistance we need without having to build, and pay for, a staff. Consultants you can get rid of and no one cares, but cutting out staff is a big deal."

Phil walked across the office and pointed to a large framed photo.

"This was a worldwide meeting held by the company I was with before Masters, as you know. This group photo has to have 250 people in it, from the chairperson down to me. It was taken 10 years before I left."

He came over and sat again.

"When I left there were only about three members of the original group remaining. Some had gone on to better things. Some had run afoul of the old man. Some were tossed out because they just didn't work out. A few went off to start their own companies. For the most part, they all have done well.

"The company had a lot of wonderfully talented people and took good care of them, but for some reason it didn't do all that well itself. Today it is a much more profitable shell of its former self, but no one likes it, inside or out."

I walked over to take a look at the photo.

"I know a lot of people in this picture, it brings back memories. You know the reason this outfit is not going strong today is that it thought it was infallible. The managers had a wonderful data system and financial controls never seen before or since. They thought all they had to do was keep track, pound down the problems, and acquire companies to fill in any cracks that might appear in a product line."

Phil cocked his head.

"Are you saying that they missed the point? They worked on the wrong things?"

"Not necessarily wrong. It's just that they didn't think about the type of characteristics that let a corporation go on forever, or if they thought about them, they didn't do anything about it. We haven't been taking them into consideration ourselves, at least not as part of our strategy. Like them, we have not been very people- or customer-oriented.

"For instance, no managers would encourage people to do things wrong the first time, but they don't do much about helping them get it done right the first time. Everyone makes changes, but very few take care to inject them into the bloodstream of the company. We all want people to be proud of their work, but we don't do much about making it happen."

Phil opened his board where the strategy plans had been written.

"As I look at what I have been working on, I see that this is not very people-oriented. It is all about finances and markets. We certainly have to concentrate on them, but they just aren't the whole nine yards."

His face brightened.

"Incidentally, I have been saying 'the whole nine yards' for years without knowing where it came from. The other day my nine-year-old announced that it referred to filling up a cement truck, which holds nine yards of cement. Apparently unethical drivers figured out that they didn't have to totally empty the truck so they could make a little money on the side dropping off a yard or so for their own benefit. So the site supervisor would warn the drivers to make sure they delivered the whole nine yards."

I patted Phil on the shoulder, asked him to keep me informed, and went back to my office. As usual, there was a list of telephone calls and a stack of mail. That would keep me out of trouble for a while. It was going to be difficult making myself let the organization work its way out of this and into the future. But there would be no future without the organization, so I had to define my personal role very carefully: keep the heat up, offer useful support, but not take charge of it.

A month later the Audit Committee met to hear Manufacturing Division President Pearl Turner, Systems Integrity Director Walter Dubow, and Manufacturing Director Lou O'Conner.

The meeting started out as usual with our guests being introduced and then Pearl taking the floor to bring us up-to-date on the status in Manufacturing concerning items that interested us. I introduced her.

"We know that you, Victor, and Phil have been involved in developing a strategy for reorienting the culture of the company, and there is no need for us to get involved in that at this time, unless you think it would be helpful to our understanding. Our main interest is in things that drain cash or resources from the company and do not produce anything in return. So please go ahead, Pearl, this is an informal session as you have already guessed."

"Thank you, George," she said. "Louis and Walter are here to help answer any questions that might be out of my area of knowledge. I thought that the clearest way to present the story would be to follow the Systems Integrity report card format. So I will go along that line.

"The first item was people doing things right the first time and, as part of that, the Price of Nonconformance. Our studies show that Masters' PONC is about the same as others in the same fields. But there is always room for improvement. Let me ask Louis to go over those numbers and their causes individually. Lou?"

O'Conner rose to his feet and moved to the foot of the table. He was a Masters veteran, having worked his way up through the years. He was an outstanding production leader. Productivity was always on his mind.

"I have gone over these numbers and would like to see if we can put them into perspective. Let me put the viewgraph up on the screen. I don't think we need the lights off; it is only for reference.

"The first category is Rework, $20 million dollars. Of course that is too high, but most of that rework is planned. Some of it, like printed circuit board touch-up, is a normal part of the manufacturing process. It really shouldn't be called rework. I have a meeting with accounting on that next week."

Al had been punching his calculator. He looked up at O'Conner and commented.

"If I figure $25,000 a year for a worker, counting benefits and everything, which is probably low, I come to the conclusion that $20,000,000 would buy the services of 800 people. Is that right?"

Lou became a little flustered.

"I'm sure the math is right, but there certainly aren't 800 people involved in rework. Usually it is spread around and is part of everyone's job. We do have some special areas, like the printed circuit board touch-up area that I mentioned."

Pearl waved her pencil in the air.

"When each process is set up, industrial engineers figure the tradeoffs between perfection and efficiency. It would be prohibitive to have processes without rework; you'd have to throw away what produces a large part of our margin. But we have improvement programs going on all the time."

Lou picked up a folder.

"We have just started a broader statistical quality control program, and we're taking another look at our equipment. I'm sure we will be able to reduce rework quite a bit as we get into it."

"The next significant item is Warranty Field Service. I checked with the accounting people, and they have listed only the field service associated with customer complaints. The normal service, for which we get paid, is not included. This is as it should be.

"Warranty by itself is $14 million of the $24 million. Field service is $10 million. Much of the warranty cost comes from design problems that we have not been able to get enough action on."

"What is the biggest single warranty problem?" asked Foster. "Is there any one or group of items that stand out?"

"I think Walter might be able to answer that a little better than I. Walt?"

"Electronic components, most of which we buy from suppliers, have been the most consistent and expensive problems. Their failure rate has been higher than the national average, so we are going to have to do something about that. These same failures have an influence on what is listed as excess inventory." Walter closed his folder and looked at Lou.

"We are not too sure about this 'excess inventory' category," said Lou. "Who's to say what inventory is too much?"

"I thought the idea was to establish a system of having little or no inventory on hand. Have we done anything about that?" I asked.

"Pete Miller, who runs purchasing, is out on the coast today," said Pearl, "but I talked with him about it. He says that they are trying to get the zero inventory program moving, but one of the problems is in components. They are able to get better prices by ordering in larger lots. That gives the impression of having excess inventory."

"Are these the same components that lead the warranty parade?" asked Al. Lou nodded and Al continued.

"Could it be that they are not sending us the good stuff because we will buy a lot of them if they give us a discount?"

"I don't know about that," replied Pearl, "but we sure do have trouble with components, among other things."

Lou changed charts on the machine.

"We think we are responsive to our customers, but are going back to look at these charges that we have not been using data received from them. Engineering is conducting a special study on it, and we should have a report by the end of the month. We will make certain that everyone gets a copy of it."

"Do you anticipate the need to change the procedure for reviewing customer data, such as warranty and field service generated information?" asked Vincent. "Will there be a whole new way of doing it?"

Lou shook his head.

"I doubt it," he said. "The system we have has been working well for a long time. We don't like to change what doesn't need changing."

"Speaking of change," I said, "how about the report card's rating of intensive care for all of us. Are we really that bad?"

Pearl smiled.

"I don't think so. Most of the items that came up had little to do with the hardware. They were primarily people problems. It is very hard to get people to read or ask about things that change. But we will be looking into it."

"And how about the pride issue?" I asked.

"I can't see where that comes from," said Pearl. "Our people are very proud of the company and their work. I would like to have Cynthia come over and spend some time with us to see if we really need to do anything. Naturally we are concerned, but I don't see it as a priority item."

Cynthia bristled.

"I'd be glad to come do another survey, but what we learned came from real people. I think it is a big problem."

Pearl smiled and nodded.

"We will certainly include it in the action report. As you all know Phil has set up sessions with Victor and myself to work up a corporatewide strategy for updating our culture. I think many of these items will be addressed during that."

"Let me get this clear in my mind, Pearl and Lou," I said. "You believe that the quality issue is exaggerated; you think that the customer is listened to; you believe that we handle change okay—it's just that the people don't listen; and you think that people are really proud to work here, and the analysis was wrong."

"I think 'wrong' is too strong a word, George, but frankly we don't see a great deal that needs to be done about it. Perhaps some more information will come out of Phil's meetings."

"But the Price of Nonconformance in Manufacturing is more than our pretax profit. I am quite concerned about it, but more concerned that the senior management does not believe there is a problem. Do you really think we can go on as is?" asked Foster.

"We are very concerned. I hope we didn't give you the impression that we aren't. But we have a large and complex organization to run. These issues are built into the fabric of our operation. We can't just hop on the quality part without doing something about the others," said Pearl.

"Well this is an information session, not an operations review," I said. "So we will let all you folks get back to work, and the Audit Committee will finish up some housekeeping matters. Thank you for coming and for your frank presentation."

Everyone got up, shook hands, and chatted with one other, and in a few minutes there were just we four directors left. We all sat quietly and and stayed that way. Finally, Foster turned to me and said: "I think I know where some of the problem lies."

"One could get that impression," I said, sadly. "But we agreed they would probably be defensive. I'll chat with Phil about it, but he has his own thing going to reset priorities. One thing we could do is ask the Insurance Division to come to us earlier. If I could set up that meeting in the next two weeks, could you all work it in?"

They all scrambled for their pocket calendars and noodled with them for a moment and then nodded in my direction.

"It's got to be more interesting than anything I've got going," said Vincent. "We have a couple of mergers going on and an enormous loan loss in Latin America, but I'd rather be here."

"Me too," said Al.

"Ditto," said Foster. "We are opening a new property at the start of next week in Dallas. But I'm sure we can work around that, one way or another."

"Okay, we're on. Meeting is over. I'll put you down for the motion to adjourn, Foster."

I went back to my office rather absentmindedly. Fortunately I made it without incident. One Sunday on our way to church I was driving the family along, chatting away, and wound up in the parking lot of the golf course, which is sort of in the same direction. When I pulled into a parking space they all just sat there and looked at me, I get reminded of it regularly.

I hadn't been back for 10 minutes before Phil came in. I greeted him and we sat at the conference table.

"I don't have to ask you how you felt about the Manufacturing presentation," he said. "It's written all over you."

"I couldn't believe it," I agreed. "I thought Pearl was more open and advanced than that. They all acted like it was nothing serious. Could it be they really don't understand? Or don't they want anything else to do right now?"

"We will find out very soon. I hope it is just a problem of needing direction and feeling defensive. I would hate to think of having to replace that entire management group at this time," said Phil.

"Don't fool around if you decide it is necessary. We can provide people with generous severance packages, so no one will be hurt—except their feelings, of course. But we can't afford to have a $100 million leak in our boat, and more importantly we can't fail to manage the company so it will survive and grow. I believe that we are really at a crossroads in our corporation, and I know you do too."

Phil got up and walked around like he always did when he was thinking about something or had a difficult decision to consider.

"You must be a lousy poker player," I said.

He blushed and grinned.

"Guilty," he said. "I just cannot hide my concern. My poker face is like a television screen. But then it also implies a boyish openness that works to my advantage," he grinned. "Seriously, I have about come to the conclusion that Pearl is just not tough or thoughtful enough. She just doesn't want to make a mistake. But I don't have any other jobs for her, or for Lou."

I walked around too.

"Why not have a 'cards on the table' chat with her? It is possible that she just needs some education and a clearer understanding of where the company is going. Can you take her to some quiet spot and talk it out?"

"Pearl is about 53 and has a two-year contract. If it becomes necessary to let her go, we could work something out to give her five years on her retirement and she could get paid as if she were 60 after having received two years of full pay. That should make up for a lot of hurt feelings, but I hope she will see the light and get with it."

"How about Lou?" he asked. "He really is a treasure in his way, but I don't think we will ever convert him."

"We may have to crack a lot of eggs in making this particular omelet. If some people are going to be let go or transferred, we want to do it in a way that will not backlash on us. People can't have pride in a company that treats anyone harshly."

"When we get further along, I'll bring Human Resources and the lawyers together to help lay out a policy, if that makes sense. But I doubt that we will have problems with more than a couple of people. The Insurance Division, for instance, knows it has to change. You are going to be pleased with its status report to the audit committee." He got up to leave.

"Oh that reminds me," I said. "Could Victor come to the Audit Committee meeting sometime in the next two weeks instead of next month? Foster has a date in Dallas on the 13th, but any other time would be okay. Could you have it arranged?"

"No problem. We'll coordinate it with Cynthia and your office."

We shook hands and he left. I couldn't help but think he was soon going to be tough enough to be CEO. It couldn't come quickly enough for me. *Tough* in this case doesn't mean beating up on people, of course. It refers to being able to stick to the necessary policies and actions no matter how enticing the reasons for easing up. The typical CEO takes office determined to reign rather than direct. However, it isn't long before it becomes clear that executives left to their own policy making will get off on a track inconsistent with the CEO's. So authority can be delegated, but only after it has been packaged.

So changing the company over was going to be something I would have to orchestrate personally, but not too obviously. I was looking forward to the Insurance meeting.

Victor Hakel and two members of his team appeared at the Audit Committee meeting on time. He had brought Systems Integrity Director Everett Walker, and Financial Director Jack Rudolph.

Victor is an outgoing person and was quite comfortable with the directors. He had managed our Atlanta branch for several years prior to moving into his present assignment. As he introduced his associates and chatted with the committee, I could see that Victor was confident about his position in the company. I envy people who can come to that conclusion. I have always been secretly afraid that someone was going to catch up with me one day. I think the moment in my life when I felt the most inadequate was when the Board elected me chief executive.

I called the meeting to order, introduced the guests, and asked if there were any questions before Victor began his presentation.

"I have just one, and I know you will be covering it. However, I can't wait," said Foster. "It is about that double payment of tax to the state. Could you relieve my curiosity, and then I won't bother you during the presentation."

Victor smiled.

"No trouble for me at all. I'm going to let Jack explain it to you. We screwed up, but the state took advantage of us."

He nodded to Jack, who was blushing and trying to look stern at the same time.

"We have an annual tax bill calculated on our business cash flow. This year it was $1 million. Some years ago the state negotiated this arrangement with the insurance companies. It protects them against being taxed on other business characteristics. It is a practical deal, and we all like it.

"However, one state senator put a rider in the bill that said if the payments were ever late, the bill would be doubled. He didn't like giving away anything to these companies.

"Well for years everyone just figured the tax and sent it in.

At one time the governor would have a luncheon and the chairpersons of the various companies would bring their tax payments to be delivered personally. It was all very festive but fell into disuse about 25 years ago."

"So what happened?" I asked. "Did the Governor not come pick up the check, or what?"

Jack blushed again.

"We mailed it to the wrong place. It got mixed up with a mail sack for an agent in New Jersey, and by the time they found it, called us to see what to do about it, and then we got it back, the time had expired."

Foster shook his head.

"Why didn't we just make out another check and hand-carry it over there? The State House is just across the park from you."

"That is just what we did, eventually, but we missed the deadline by a day. It never occurred to us that they would seriously enforce the letter of the law. After all, we have a lot of employees there. But they insisted, and we had to lay out $1 million, cash."

"What action has been taken to make certain we don't have this problem any more?" asked Al.

Jack started to answer, but Victor interrupted.

"We will obviously get the tax checks out earlier. Also we have been looking into the mail system, and we find that it is a tragic situation. Our people have been actually taking company mail down to the post office themselves and paying for it out of their own pocket in order to mail things they consider important. The manager has been replaced, and a top to bottom shake-up is in progress. Everyone will get a message out of that."

"Have you defined the message you want them to get?" I asked.

Victor looked puzzled.

"Not to take things for granted, I suppose," he said. "I was just using a phrase when I said they would get a message. But to answer your question, I guess we didn't really think that out. I will make certain we do it all properly."

He glanced around the room.

"Shall we proceed with our presentation?"

Everyone settled in, so Victor began.

"We have been studying the ESO analysis, and I have to say that in general we agree completely. The differences we have are minor, so actually we accept the review as it is. Cynthia and her gang have done a fine job in showing us how to look at our operation differently.

"And as we look at it, we see a business that has a lot of problems. Most of them are under our own control; a few rest in the nature of the beast. There are people we have difficulty in influencing, like independent agents. Interest rates have a mind of their own, and the competition pushes us into areas we sometimes would really not like to visit.

"However, we are going to turn it around. Let's take a look at some of the problems and their causes. That will give you a good idea of what has to happen. Phil, Pearl, and I are having a session later this week to get into the specifics. Pearl is very excited about the opportunity for improvement in Manufacturing."

"Pearl?" I mumbled.

Victor blinked, paused, and then motioned to Harry Sanders.

Harry moved to the flip chart and turned to the first drawing.

"As we look at the expense numbers here, we see what we are wasting money on, in this case reprocessing. Back in my manufacturing days, we would have called this rework. But there is more than a word change involved.

"In Manufacturing most rework is due to one of three things: quality of work, component failure, and wrong engineering information. But in the paperwork-computer world there are many more causes to choose from. We actually have a great deal more rework in Insurance than they do in in Manufacturing. Theirs runs about $5000 per employee; ours is over $16,000 each. Our mistakes are much more expensive to fix. Chasing electrons around software and wires is a bigger deal than resoldering a component."

Al was doing some figuring.

"So if I look at the overall nonconformance costs, I see that Manufacturing, counting lost sales, runs around $28,000 per person and Insurance is $42,000. Those sound like average total compensation and benefits. In essence we are paying everyone twice?"

Victor shook his head.

"I don't think it is that bad. Remember many of these costs are just part of doing business. Our people are just as effective as anyone else in the industry."

"Victor," I said. "How about giving us the ESO rating your staff came up with for the Insurance Division? Perhaps we can get a better picture before we start through the numbers and their causes."

"Sure, no problem," he replied, and Harry turned a few pages on the flip chart.

INSURANCE DIVISION ESO RATING

People do things right routinely.   = Healing

Growth is profitable and steady.   = Wellness

Customer needs are the priority.   = Healing

Change is planned and managed. = Healing

People are proud to work there.   = Wellness

"Don't you have a 30 percent turnover rate throughout the division?" I asked. "And isn't $9 million of your nonconformance cost due to salespeople turnover alone?"

"True," said Victor, slightly puzzled.

"Then how do you get a 'wellness' on people being proud to work there? I would think the turnover would be zero in order to get that evaluation."

"Well it depends on how you look at it, George," said Victor. "Most of the two-way traffic is at the lower level of the organization. People change jobs for a few more bucks a week across the street. We can hardly be expected to match each of those. It would be like paying greenmail. We manage it all and get very few complaints from the employees about it."

He motioned for the presentation to continue.

As it droned on, I was getting a tight feeling in my tummy. It was beginning to become clear to me that these people did not attach the slightest significance to these ESO ratings. As far as they could see, it was just another senior staff exercise in meaninglessness. We were going to have to do something to help them really recognize the seriousness involved. Otherwise, the corporation was headed for problems. The way we managed was destructive.

10

Discovering Wellness

Phil, Pearl, and Victor assembled in Phil's office for their long-planned strategy session.

"I'll go get the coffee," said Phil. He went out to the coffee area and brought back three cups. Putting them around the table, he noted that it was easy to do the job when everyone took coffee black.

"I used to pretend not to drink coffee," said Pearl. "Then no one would expect me to go get it. But I have gotten over that, and it doesn't bother me to have the president tote and fetch for me."

Phil smiled.

"We seem to have become comfortable with the female executive now, but it must have caused some interesting situations in the past," he said.

Pearl waved her hand.

"It isn't over yet. People still think I'm my secretary when I call them, so I don't get to do impact calling like you guys."

"'Impact calling?'" said Victor. "That is a new one on me, what is that?"

Pearl patted him on the arm.

"I can't believe you are that innocent, Victor," noted Pearl. "But that is when you call a subordinate, supplier, customer, or such directly. They pick up the phone and there you are in all your importance. They don't expect it; therefore it makes an impact. Sort of gives you the advantage."

"I'll have to try that," said Victor, "but I have trouble just getting people to return my calls now."

Phil shuffled his papers around, and the others turned to positioning themselves to listen.

"We are together to talk about strategy, which is an overworked word, as we all know. So I thought I would see if I could make clear what I mean by it and what I think the chairman is looking for."

"He certainly is wound up in this 'eternally successful' business," said Pearl. "My session with the Audit Committee was the longest afternoon of my life. Isn't it kind of unusual for one Board committee to become that involved with operations?"

"I was wondering about that too," said Victor. "They really are getting into things."

"My understanding is that they are not interested in operations as such," said Phil. "They are more concerned with whether we are meeting the objectives of the company. That is why they had the ESO audit conducted.

"This all fits in with our overall strategy of running the company. If everything is positioned correctly and we are working on the right things, then the company runs the way we want it. Otherwise, we just go from day to day, patching and fixing."

"Sort of like we are doing now?" asked Victor.

"Sort of like we are doing now," replied Phil.

"But it is a tough old world out there," said Pearl, "to coin a phrase. We can't just lay out some master scheme, mail it to everyone, and then wait for success to fly home."

"True, true. However, we have a choice about where things are going," said Phil, rising to his feet. "We don't have to just let the tides take us. We can set up our own wellness strategy."

"I'm learning all kinds of new words today. What has *wellness* to do with corporate strategy? I usually associate that with aerobic workouts or dieting," said Victor.

"Also true. But the wellness I am talking about refers to the actions we take in order to avoid not being sick. For instance, we all agree that we have to take dramatic action to deal with the Price of Nonconformance numbers."

"Dramatic is right," said Pearl. "We are sending all 4000 employees through the Quality College courses so they can learn to prevent. Starting Monday, I am spending a week I can ill afford in class so I can understand my personal role in what is called 'making quality happen.' I am resigned to all this. We will be involved in quality improvement the rest of our days. It takes a lot to change attitudes, but we already see results. There are a lot of things that people can do when they think management is interested. Frankly, I have been pleasantly surprised."

"Prevent is a good word for it," said Phil. "The idea of wellness is that if we had taken the concern and the actions necessary to prevent problems with quality, we would not have to be going through this improvement process. It doesn't cost much in itself, but we spent a fortune doing things wrong and now we have to spend a lot of time getting well."

Victor nodded.

"I don't have any problem understanding that at all. We obviously dropped the ball. When we don't have to use up computer time debugging programs, we have what amounts to a 30 percent increase in capacity. That becomes easy to see once someone belts you across the head with the proof.

"But there are a lot of things we can't do much about. We have to separate the strategy objectives into categories if we are going to hold management responsible for everything. The next thing you know our incentive compensation will be divided into five equal portions of quality, growth, customers, change, and pride. Chaos will reign."

Pearl shook her head.

"You mean you want a Chinese menu management responsibility strategy—two from column A and three from column B? You know better than that Victor."

She was obviously irritated, and Phil was surprised at her

emotion. Usually Pearl was slow to take the initiative on anything that was the slightest bit subjective. One of the things she liked about manufacturing was that it produced real things, not just data.

Victor blushed, but didn't back down.

"Obviously we cannot evade any responsibility for the whole package. I agree to that. What I am concerned with is the anticipation of what we would be expected to accomplish. If we are going to be pioneers, we need to get it documented."

He rose from his chair and walked over to lean on the corner of Phil's desk.

"Take this business of 'The employees are proud to work here.' Now I know that it is important, as we all do. But making it happen can be well beyond what even a division president can pull off. There are many considerations, like the pension program, for instance, that are set by others. I'm just saying that we have to be careful."

Now Phil was becoming sensitive.

"I think you are being somewhat parochial, Victor. Our mission is to lay out the beginning of a strategy to make the company eternally successful. Everyone would be involved, and if employee benefit programs are part of that, then so be it. We will not be expecting miracle-working.

"But," he cautioned, "it is going to have to be a different approach from what we now have. At present we are not very people-oriented, and success is measured only by financial returns. We have to keep on with that, but employees and customers have to receive proper attention."

Pearl was becoming more concerned.

"A complete change of culture could really be hard for some of our people to accept. My folks are very hard to change. Lou O'Conner, for instance. He produces like no one else, but he has missed the last two revolutions. It is going to take more than a grand plan, setting up teams and having culture classes. What you are talking about, Philip, is rearranging real life. You want a whole new world, not just a new deal."

"How are we going to get our suppliers to cooperate?" asked Victor. "I am really concerned about them."

"Let's wait and see what they have to cooperate about," said Phil, patiently. "Then we can worry about it. Right now I would like to get back to the subject at hand, which is corporate wellness." Everyone nodded, and Phil continued.

"When an individual goes to a personal wellness center, the first thing that happens is the creation of a personal profile. Bodily characteristics, blood chemistry, mental positioning, and behavior patterns are all laid out. Then the computer program predicts the future life and health span of the individual based on all that data. If you have never had it done, I recommend it. It can be quite startling."

Victor was interested.

"You mean that they get very specific? They tell you that you will live to be 55 doing what you now do, and that you could make 80 if you forgo your wicked ways?"

Phil nodded.

"You got it. Very specific."

"And that is what you want to do with Masters?" asked Pearl. "You and George are really serious about all this, aren't you? I mean, you really think this company can be restructured so that it meets the criteria for wellness?"

"In a word, yes. We think there is no other choice," said Phil. "The world changes too fast for us to continue as we have for all this time."

"Masters has done well," said Victor.

"Every year has been a battle," replied Phil. "And every year in the future will also be a battle, but we need to have a managerial purpose that gives us a permanent edge over the others. We can't get surprised like we were a few years ago when the Japanese appeared in our market out of nowhere."

"And we can't continue spending all that money doing things wrong on purpose." stated Pearl. "I think I am beginning to get with it. I don't mind saying that I have been a little negative about this whole thrust up to now. I'm sure George was thinking over how to put me out to pasture during my Audit Committee comments."

There was a short silence.

Phil turned to Victor.

"What do you think about all this?" he asked.

"Well, I'm all for getting better, and since I've got 25 or so years to work, I would much prefer to do it in a company that is going to be here and be successful.

"The only problem I am having is that I don't want to get all wrapped up in the traditional ways of making quick improvement. I realize that the quality thing, for instance, is going to require a companywide education and implementation process. It is a cultural change in that it is an information bank change. People are learning a different and more effective way of dealing with a subject.

"In this ESO approach we are talking about entirely different behavior throughout the managerial process. We are creating a new civilization."

Phil was impressed.

"You are certainly on the right track. I think many of these five characteristics will be dealt with individually, and yet they will be handled all at the same time also."

Pearl stood up and moved across the room.

"If you guys are going to walk around for the next several hours, I might as well get up too. We are going to have to involve other people in this and perhaps ask for advice from someone who has experience in making all this happen."

Victor sat down.

"Well we already have a consulting firm helping us with 'People to do things right routinely,' which I believe is the first characteristic we want to implement. Incidentally, I think that pulling this one off would solve about half of the problems involved in the other four."

He got back up again and began to pace.

"'Growth,'" he put two fingers in the air, "'that is profitable and steady,' is the result of good strategic direction. It is a matter of knowing the market. So we will probably need some marketing and financial help in that one."

"'Customer needs are the priority,'" said Pearl, "refers more to new products than anything else, if I read it right.

After all, we satisfy customers' needs only if we give them what they want, or can use, which, I hope, is the same thing."

"That is a very tricky area. People spend fortunes on it and come up blank."

"'Change is planned and managed,' is something we have begun to work on internally by developing Systems Integrity. I think we can handle this one ourselves," said Phil.

"So that leaves 'People are proud to work here,'" said Victor. "To me that is potentially the most difficult part of this whole thing. People are hard to figure sometimes. Who knows what makes them proud?"

"Well we know a lot of things that pull them in the opposite direction," said Pearl. "I suspect eliminating those items would be a big step. We must drive them nuts with our up-and-down operations. The health-care insurance program is not all that terrific, and there are a few other problem areas. However, the big item—to me anyway—is that we don't let them know what to be proud about."

Phil was beginning to think there was some hope after all.

"I agree we have not given a great deal of thought to those things, and we certainly have not asked the people for their input. We must do that in the future.

"Right now I would like to see if we can work up a plan for coping with all this. We need to get the goals straight, enlist the participation of the executives and managers, and then take it all to the people. We have the full support of the Board, and resources will not be a problem.

"However, there are two aspects: first, this has to become an ongoing thing—it can't be some program that disappears in a few months like the usual ones; second, we have to get moving—every day we take is a day the company slips a bit more down the embankment."

"We could call this 'up the embankment,'" said Victor.

"Or 'be nice to everyone or die,'" offered Phil.

"How about 'capitalism at its best'?" said Pearl.

"Whatever it is, we have a big task. I suggest that we work up a short letter of intent that we can show to George and use as a working guide at the next level meetings," said Phil.

"Part of that should be a listing of the five ESO characteristics and a grade of 'Intensive Care' beside each one. That
way no one will think they are any better at one than another," suggested Pearl.

"I think that would be a good start," said Victor. "Both divisions as well as headquarters will then be the same, and we
can head off any defensiveness by the staffs."

"Good," said Phil. "Now speaking of staffs, we will want to
get them involved in the strategy. I suggest that we make
Cynthia the chairperson of a team to lay out the implementation process. Each of you assign two people, and we will
have two from headquarters. After they are finished, we will
all be able to lay out our personal roles and get started."

Both nodded in agreement and said they would select the
team members before leaving the meeting.

"Let's get to work on our letter," said Phil, and they bent to
the task.

TO: George Kale

FROM: Philip Moore, Pearl Turner, Victor Hakel
    cc: Cynthia Elliott, Leroy Carrell, David Statham, Harry
    Sanders, Everett Walker, Walter Dubow, Donald Hoffamn

SUBJ.:   Eternally Successful Organization strategy.

We feel that it is vital to the future of our corporation to establish a deliberate operating strategy that will result in Masters'
employees and resources being utilized to make the corporation
successful eternally. This strategy must be based on firm principles and yet be flexible enough to manage the requirements
of the future.

The basis of the strategy is as follows:

▪ People do things right routinely.

    (At present there is an organized effort to install a qual-
ity improvement process to change this from what we have
been experiencing. The measurement of success is the Price of
Nonconformance. Once we have recovered, the problem will be
to make this the normal attitude of the company.)

▪ Growth is profitable and steady.

(We need to set a percentage growth goal [15 percent?] so the company will always be large enough to compete properly; an income goal [12 percent after tax] so the company will have a strong and positive cash flow that will reduce the need for debt, a debt-to-equity ratio [1 to 4?] that will preclude financial strain during times of economic uncertainty, and an acquisition analysis effort that will keep us from getting involved in businesses we do not understand.)

- Customer needs are anticipated.

(We need a continuous evaluation and research activity that lets us know what customers are looking for, a product development effort keyed to that research, and executive awareness of the sensitivity of the issues.)

- Change is planned and managed.

(The Systems Integrity concept provides a focal point for planning change, but the key is executive awareness of the inevitability of change and the absolute necessity of making certain that everyone understands and implements it.)

- People are proud to work there.

(This has to be the result of a genuine environment, not just a motivational device. It has to be established, not created. Employee participation is vital in putting the establishment together.)

This letter will serve as direction to the team listed above, who will be laying out the implementation process. We will bring you all together when you are ready to discuss your status.

11

Cynthia's Committee

"This letter will serve as direction...." Don Hoffman tossed the memo on the table. "I have heard of some screwy adventures, but this has to be the strangest. I think they have really flipped out this time."

"Huh?" said Cynthia.

"Don is not the most positive person in the world, Cynthia. You'll just have to get used to it," said Walter. "Why do you think this is an adventure, Donald?"

"Because it is not doable, at least not for more than a moment or two anyway. It's like landing on the moon, walking around a little, and then coming back—nothing left but a few empty beer cans and some chilly memories."

"You think we couldn't create something that will last?" asked Cynthia. "We ought to at least give it a thought, anyway."

Somehow she was not feeling quite as sure of herself as when she was discussing the concepts with Phil and George.

"Well we're going to have some time with Mr. Kale today, so you can tell him all about your reservations," said David Statham. "We need to be sure we all understand the objectives the same way, and having worked with our chairperson before, I can guarantee we will."

Harry Sanders came into the conference room and greeted each member of the team.

"Being late for the first meeting is not setting a very good example," he said. "However, I have a wonderful excuse if anyone is interested in hearing it. I was trying to convince the finance department that they can't unilaterally change forms without telling anyone."

"I thought that was all put to bed," said Cynthia. "Honestly, some of these departments are so stubborn."

"It's all taken care of, chief. At least this time, it is. I can see why the old man wants us to change the way we do business. People are really out for themselves. They don't think about the company as a whole."

"My observations exactly," said Don. "That is why it will take a complete brain transplant to change this outfit. A few policies and teams will not affect anything."

"It's time to go see Mr. Kale," Walter reminded the others.

"Let's go," said Cynthia. "We're meeting in the board-room."

The seven of them wound their way through the halls and took an elevator to the 16th floor.

"This is just the right size for a committee," said Everett. "Any bigger and we wouldn't fit in the same elevator."

"It could take weeks to decide how to divide the group in order to take two or three cars," said Don. "Committees are not known for making decisions."

"The men at the Constitutional Convention managed, Don. And they were talking about more important things than we are. There is a solution to everything if we want to work at it," replied Cynthia.

She was getting a little tired of his negativism. However, she reminded herself that they had to come up with a plan that took care of all eventualities, and Don was one of those eventualities. So she smiled and patted him on the shoulder.

"Perhaps we should all go to Philadelphia to work on this."

"Please," commented Don.

When they entered the boardroom, Phil and I were waiting for them.

"Have a cup of coffee," I said cheerfully, "I'm glad you

could all join us. Just take a seat anywhere. Cynthia, sit over here at the head of the table. Then we'll give you the bill."

As they all settled down I walked to the side of the room and opened the wall panel that hid the marker board.

"In case we come up with anything that needs to be written, we can use this board. Somehow, though, this room is more conducive to thinking and conversation than to writing.

"I am pleased that you have agreed to join in this task. Let me be very clear in saying that we do not expect you to put together some miracle-oriented system that is going to leap-frog existing managerial knowledge. Companies don't go from 'Comatose' to 'Wellness' in a few weeks. Not that we have that far to come. The things we are talking about doing are not all that complicated, and for the most part the ways to accomplish them are known.

"They do not get done routinely because prevention is not in keeping with the systems and priorities we have been raised to think are important. The theme of wellness is what we have to emphasize and learn to take as normal."

I walked back to the board and wrote the word *wellness* in large letters across the middle of the white panel.

"We have to stop doing the things that make us sick and start doing the things that keep us healthy and prosperous. As Woody Allen said once, at least I think it was Woody Allen: 'It is better to be rich and healthy than to be poor and sick.'"

They all laughed politely, each of them wondering silently how all this was ever going to come off. I sensed this and went back to my chair and sat down. This was going to take some doing. I continued anyway.

"We are giving you the concepts and overall direction. What we need you to provide is the implementation process. All of you are closer to the operations and the people than we are. If you can think out the flow and figure how to get these concepts imbedded into Masters, then we will take it from there. Phil and I will drive the process personally."

I paused and looked around the room, inviting questions or comments on what had transpired so far.

David Statham leaned forward.

"I have spent most of my career in Marketing, as you know, George, and I have seen some wonderful ideas that never got anywhere because of the way they were presented. Those with true substance come around eventually, but that is as much luck as anything else."

I nodded encouragingly, which is one of my better traits.

"The key to anything like we are going to try is a clear identification for the individuals involved of what is in it for them," he continued. "Are we promising eternal employment, continual dividends, a work-free environment? What has to occur to get people to actually make all this happen? Those are some of the things we have to clarify."

"Any 'jobs for life' sort of attempt comes back to bite you. The Japaneese found that out," said Don.

I was beginning to lose a little of my enthusiasm for this approach. Consensus management was never one of the things I selected as the way to run a company. I realize that everyone has to have an input, and I have come to believe in the face of conventional wisdom that committees often make the best decisions. However it is hard to select the right people who can look at the job objectively. Everyone has a secret agenda, and some cannot place it on the back burner when required.

"I don't think we are talking about new social concepts," I said. "We do things to ourselves that make corporate health vulnerable. It really is just like the personal concept. If you do harmful things to yourself, your life span gets shorter. If you don't do those things, then you live longer. We need to translate that into the corporation."

"We can't solve all these things here," said Cynthia. "As we go along, we will come up with questions for you and Phil. Can we count on your participation on a regular basis?"

"Absolutely," said Phil. "We would sit in each session if we didn't think it would be depressing for you. We need to get a broad view of how to approach the implementation process."

"Then it is already agreed that we are going to try to make a change along these lines?" asked David. "How are we going to make changes out in the regions? They are going to need a lot of personal attention."

"We'll have to provide that," replied Phil. "I suspect there will be several problems of communication we will have to approach in a unique way. But we have good old-fashioned closed circuit TV to help us along, as well as training resources."

"Does anyone else have any questions at this time?" asked Cynthia. When there was no response, both Phil and I began to leave.

"We are available whenever you need us. I hope you will be able to give us a starting point in a couple of weeks. Good luck," Phil said, and we left.

It was about three weeks later that Cynthia asked to see me and told me that she wanted to disband the implementation team.

"What do you mean you want to disband the group?" I asked. Actually I yelled, if the truth were known.

"What do you mean they will never get anything done? We set them up with a clear charter, in writing. We gave them top management access and support. We provided an opportunity to be famous.

"According to the management books that should make it a cinch. What is happening?"

She motioned for me to sit down and sat calmly, hands in lap, until I plopped onto the couch.

"This is too big a change," she sighed. "No one with a functional responsibility can get too far away from it. They just cannot think about the corporation as a whole and forget what they do for a living.

"The Human Resources people see this as having an effect on the nice neat compensation and benefit programs they have installed; Marketing goes into shock about how to do research; Systems Integrity is afraid that there will be so many changes it won't be able to keep them controlled. It goes on.

"I wouldn't ask to set this group aside if there were any hope. I call us 'the little committee that wouldn't.' We need a new group and a new chairperson."

She was very disturbed.

I thought about it for a moment. I was disappointed but not too surprised. This was just one pothole along the road. It would have to be filled in and eliminated.

"We don't need a new chairperson," I said, "but we do need a new team. I suppose I knew all along that this wasn't something that could be pushed down into the organization. Some would be very uncomfortable making those kinds of decisions and then having to go back and live with their peers.

"So we'll set up a new team with you, Phil, myself, Pearl, and Victor. We'll ask Foster to sit in with us when he can as a sort of consultant. He has a great eye for the impractical."

She was nodding along with me, and I could see that her composure had returned from its brief trip off to wherever it drifts off on us.

"We could call this group TLTC: 'The little team that could,'" she offered. "And I would suggest that we take each characteristic one at a time, before putting them all together. This is a very complex concept; it will work, but we have to understand it.

"Also there is one thing I would like us all to do."

"What is that?" I asked.

"Well, it might sound silly but I think it would help if we all went to the hospital Wellness Clinic and had individual profiles made on ourselves. It would help us all understand what the concepts are we are trying to put forth."

I wasn't too sure this was all necessary, and the helpful part was not completely clear.

"What will we understand that we don't know now?" I asked.

"I think we will all know better what wellness really is," she said. "Right now we understand it intellectually but we haven't internalized it."

"Internalized?"

She smiled, uncomfortably.

"Just getting it inside where we live, I guess. It is a new word in the management education books," she replied.

"I'll go along with it, and I think we can talk the rest of the team into it, except Foster perhaps. But after it is all over, if it does what you want, then we should be prepared to give the corporation the same test."

She brightened.

"You mean describe a profile for a business in the same format as that for a person? That would be neat. That is a word my daughter uses. Okay, I'll take that task on personally."

We both rose, and she moved toward the door, then turned back to offer her hand.

"Thanks boss. I was very worried about this, and I appreciate your consideration. We are going to solve this problem, and I am glad to be part of it."

She turned and went out. I started calling the new team members. They were delighted to join the venture and agreed to go to the wellness center when scheduled, including Foster. Pearl's operation had made a sizable donation to the center when it was formed, so she agreed to see if the appointments could be set up during the following week at our individual convenience.

I had to admit that I was not looking forward to doing this. I keep myself in pretty good shape and weigh about the same as I did when I graduated from college. However everyone else was enthusiastic about the venture, so I went along as cheerfully as possible.

Since it was coming down to the point of actually doing something, I thought that I should read the information Cynthia supplied from the center. I'm glad I did. I thought I understood the thing, but there is a great deal more to it than had crossed my mind. The key point comes down to the idea that good health is not something that just occurs, nor is it a gift from heaven. The managerial actions necessary to produce it are not automatically known to us. As far as I can see, running a body is a perfect analogy for running a business.

The risks which contribute to poor health are such things as cardiovascular disease and diabetes. But the managerial situations that cause such risks and make us vulnerable to the problems they cause are easy to understand:

- Smoking
- High blood pressure

- High cholesterol
- HDL cholesterol
- Triglycerides
- Body composition (too much fat)
- Inactive lifestyle
- Diet
- Stress control

There are others we can't do much about, like age, sex (men are higher risks), family history, and personal history. The risk of disease can be reduced by proper management. Fiber in the diet, for instance, reduces the incidence of colonic cancer. Liver problems are caused by alcohol in many cases. So the idea is to be sensible about that complicated organization that is our body and mind. We can learn to manage it rather than just react to problems all the time.

Taking the time to prevent is hard to justify in the mind of a busy person. Providing original solutions to complex problems is a lot more interesting than not having the problem in the first place. That has always been the difficulty about selling prevention. If the problem isn't there at that moment, then people assume it will not be there tomorrow or the next day. And the rewards for successful prevention just aren't there. It is hard to recognize what didn't happen and the reason for it.

The instructions from the center said not to eat anything for 12 hours before the examination, to appear in comfortable clothes, and to keep the enclosed food diary for three days before the big event. That gave me some problems. I hate diaries, even when they are for a good cause. But my wife latched onto it eagerly and kept rigorous track of everything that passed my lips. So I appeared at the appointed time fully equipped, confident my blood pressure would be off the scale.

The receptionist took my diary and helped me complete the vital information, assured me that I could have a cup of coffee as soon as the blood was drawn, and walked me to the laboratory for that purpose. The technician, George Smith, painlessly (for him) drew the specimen and instructed me where to go to produce another one.

A cheerful young woman who introduced herself as Betsy Palmer led me back to the main exercise area. People of all sizes and shapes were earnestly pumping bicycles, rowing machines, and other exercise equipment. I was particularly interested in two men who had wires taped to their chests.

"They are heart patients," said Betsy. "We can monitor them while they are doing their exercises. The gentleman on the left had a quintuple heart bypass last month. He comes in every morning to do his workout."

"I would suspect that a person with an experience like that would not have to be coaxed into this program," I said.

"You'd be surprised. A year after they have recovered from heart surgery many of them are back into their old lifestyle. They suffer for it, too, but habits are hard to change. We want to help people learn what is right for them personally so they can make it a way of life. Actually it is more comfortable and a lot more fun to live this way than to slog around all the time."

We went to a corner of the workroom, and she asked me to sit while she took my blood pressure and pulse and had me breathe into the lung capacity machine. I don't smoke, but I could see that moving the little needle would be difficult for anyone with something going into the lungs besides air.

She weighed me and then measured my body fat with a pair of calipers.

"Some centers put people in a tank of water in order to do this. It is a lot more interesting, but we learned that this way is just as accurate. Now I'd like to have you sit here on the floor in front of this bench. It has a yardstick on it, and the idea is to bend forward as far as you can. Do it easy at first. It is like trying to touch your toes, but easier to measure."

I didn't do too well on this one. Touching my toes was never something high on my list of desirable activities.

"Now I'd like to put you on this stationary bike, and we'll

check your exercise pulse and blood pressure. We'd like to get your heart up to 120 beats a minute. If at any time you feel uncomfortable, please let me know."

A young man in a jogging suit came over and introduced himself.

"I'm Doctor Watson," he said.

"Elementary," I replied.

"I have often thought of changing my name," he sighed, "but I guess it is too late now. I'll be right here in the room Mr. Kale. This is a very light test, and you are obviously in good shape, but if you have any difficulty please speak up." He checked the way my feet were mounted and nodded.

Betsy strapped the blood pressure machine on me and indicated that I should begin peddling. Periodically she would adjust the tension on the machine, check my pulse, and read the blood pressure indicator. I was beginning to drag a little, but she kept smiling and encouraging me onward. In a few moments it was all over, and I sat down to rest.

Dr. Watson sat beside me and observed me as I cooled off. "Why don't we stroll around while you cool down? People, like race horses, do better if they don't go from action to nothing right away," he said.

I agreed and we walked through the center. There is nothing like putting on a sweat suit and watching other folks work out to make you feel like a real athlete.

He showed me the lap pool, the weight room, the whirlpool bath, and all the other equipment necessary for a modern wellness center.

"By having this operation as part of the hospital we are able to provide individuals with counseling and guidance that helps make wellness a normal part of their life.

"We will have a report ready for you in a few days and will ask you to come back while we go over it together. At that time we will arrange for you to be advised by the appropriate specialists. There are several of them, and many specialize in one or two areas. For instance, almost everyone needs to talk to the diet counselor. That is something no one learned to do right."

I agreed with that.

"As far as I know, my family never gave much thought to what we should and should not eat. We just had whatever tasted good that we could afford," I said. "And regular exercise was not part of life for adults. I can remember when my father turned 45. Our family doctor told him it was time to start taking elevators; walking up the stairs was dangerous to his heart."

Watson nodded. "That is why many of our older people are not as healthy as they should be. The communicable diseases that used to reduce the population have been contained for the most part. So people live longer, but they don't necessarily have the active lives they could have.

"Also we see heart disease hitting people at younger times in life. Stress is our second most popular counseling item. Actually stress is good for us. It is how we handle it that makes the difference."

"You can teach handling stress?" I asked, amazed.

"Sure. Once people begin to recognize what can be done, they get a much better handle on it. Most of the stress we face is something we cause ourselves," he replied.

"You never ran a public company, Doctor," I said, patting him on the shoulder. "Believe me, a lot of stress comes in over the phone and in the papers."

"I'm certain that is true," he said. "But all this is another way to remove some of the stress the stockholders might cause. Look at this chart over here. It says that nonsmokers have 30 percent fewer health claims than smokers; people of average weight have 40 percent fewer claims than those who are 20 percent overweight; employees with normal blood pressure have half the claims of those whose pressure is high; and people who exercise regularly are one-third less likely to have health-care needs.

"So it is just good business to get them interested in taking care of themselves."

He smiled and turned me back to Betsy, who took my vital signs one more time and signed me out. We made an appointment at the same time next week for my readout.

I went back resolved that we were going to start our culture change by having every employee in the corporation become exposed to the value of wellness. There must be a film on the subject somewhere. We could show that and try to generate interest. We could get these folks to set up our own center or centers.

On an impulse I called the Human Resources department and talked to the health insurance manager. You learn to do this very carefully when you are chairperson. The wrong inflection in the voice can send people off after a whole new version of whatever they do.

In this case John Williams was glad to hear from me. He had, as a matter of fact, been talking to our health-care carrier just recently on the subject of wellness commitment. The information he received showed that we could probably reduce our health-care policy fees by at least 25 percent and even cut them in half if our incidents dropped. The insurance company's experience had shown that the change could occur in as few as two years. Of course, it took a few years of experience in order to reap the benefits in terms of reduced premiums.

I asked him to do some more checking and make a recommendation to the Executive Committee. He said he would do that right away.

My confidence was beginning to return.

12

The Strategy

"I want to tell you that I got the shock of my life," said Pearl. "I have had my last bit of cholesterol that can be held on a fork or in the hand. I have dropped it 10 percent in the first 10 days. I never knew my eating habits were so bad, I really just never paid attention to all that."

"Does it require a really big change?" asked Victor. "I mean do you have to eat only vegetables or something?"

"No, it is more learning what not to do. For instance, my mother insists on serving me liver, even though I don't really care for it. Every time we go to her house, I get liver. Well, the all-time champion cholesterol container is liver. Three and a half ounces have 438 milligrams of the stuff. Next in line is something I eat every morning because I can't think of anything else to prepare: eggs. Every egg has 274 milligrams. Shellfish and beef are right up there too. It is a tough list."

"So it isn't a matter of doing; it is not doing?" asked Cynthia. "By eliminating or reducing those foods, you should be able to drop the level of cholesterol in your system?"

"It will be a big help. There is also another side to the coin; there is a 'good' cholesterol. It wants to be high in order to be properly useful. That is the good news; the bad news is that the key way to make it high is to exercise regularly," lamented Pearl. "I like to walk, but the thought of putting on a leotard and leaping about the floor do not turn me on."

"Walking is the best exercise there is," I said. "The exercise counselor told me that. But it has to be a pace of 3 miles an hour, or enough to get the heart up to 120 rpm or so."

"RPM?" asked Cynthia.

"Revolutions per minute," replied Foster. "Actually he means heartbeats. RPM is about engines. But the heart is a very efficient engine, so we probably can learn to use that designation."

"What are you going to do differently, Foster?" asked Victor. "I know that I have to lose 25 pounds, most of which I put on after I quit smoking."

"That is very encouraging, Victor," said Foster. "I am going to have to quit smoking; they finally have convinced me, but the plan is to do it without gaining weight. I think they tie you in the cellar after you finish the first helping. Anyway they assure me that their plan will help me not to gain weight."

"It sounds like fantasy land, but I am sure that if it can be done, those people know how to make it happen," said Cynthia. "And speaking of fantasy land I think it is time we get started on our assignment. We need a plan of attack. I have one to suggest but am more than happy to hear a better one."

Everyone took a place around the table and listened. Cynthia lifted a folder from her briefcase.

"When we start thinking about the eternally successful characteristics, a lot of actions come to mind. There could be an endless list of things to do. It would be possible to bury an organization in all these worthwhile things to the point that nothing else got done."

Lots of heads nodded in agreement. Everyone was secretly afraid that the search for a new culture could harm the old. Masters could become like the African nations who had centuries of old customs and habits wrenched from them and replaced with impractical regulations created by a far-off government.

"Yet we have to change," she continued. "The world demands it. We cannot compete forever as we are. We have to become more efficient and reliable.

"What I am going to suggest is that we do two things: first, we discuss the thought that the ESO characteristics represent good corporate health and we should be able to list the basic actions to be taken under each of them in order to cause them to be part of Masters' operations.

"Second, we recognize that most of our problems are caused by management action, or lack of it. We make up a list of things that we will not do, things that cause us not to be healthy."

"We could put the company through a wellness test," said Victor. "That makes sense."

"Do you have something started along that line, Madam Chairperson?" I asked.

"Yes," she said. "Each of you contributed your thoughts on each characteristic, and I put in some of my own. The idea was just to try to frame the task with some do's and don't's. It is only a beginning, but we need to start somewhere."

She distributed the sheets, and we all began to read.

THE ETERNALLY SUCCESSFUL ORGANIZATION WORKSHEET

PEOPLE ROUTINELY DO THINGS RIGHT THE FIRST TIME.

Do:	Do Not:
• Educate all employees on the concepts of quality management and their role in making quality happen.	• Permit the use of "quality level" planning.
• Release and live a policy that says: We will deliver defect-free products and services to our customers, internal as well as external, on time.	• Let any person be uneducated concerning quality.
• Establish Systems Integrity operations to help organizations have a continuous evaluation of status.	• Accept deviations or waivers of agreed requirements.
• Appreciate those people and organizations who routinely meet this objective.	• Reward error-oriented behavior.

GROWTH IS PROFITABLE AND STEADY.

Do:

- Educate people to understand the basic strategy and goals of the growth program.

- Base development of new products and services on demonstrated need.

- Acquire only operations that pay their own way at the time of acquisition.

- Conduct a Systems Integrity analysis of each growth step to make certain an actual process exists

Do Not:

- Plan on synergy making a unit more profitable than it was prior to acquisition.

- Put your faith in a solitary inventor.

- Use your own cash to buy something.

- Treat the acquired people differently from your own.

CUSTOMER NEEDS ARE ANTICIPATED.

Do:

- Educate people about the proper way to listen to and understand customers, both internal and external.

- Develop an objective customer research system and review its findings formally on a continual basis.

- Monitor customer satisfaction through Systems Integrity and insist that operations perform corrective action, when indicated.

- Encourage senior management to develop personal relationships with customers.

Do Not:

- Assume that customers will stay loyal.

- Let people speak ill of the customer.

- Take advantage of the customer for any reason.

- Forget the internal customers.

CHANGE IS PLANNED AND MANAGED.

Do:

- Educate people on the concepts of change management and its advantages to them in performing their jobs.

Do Not:

- Permit people to make changes for the sake of change.

Do:	Do Not:
• Establish Systems Integrity as the central point of communications concerning change management and configuration control.	• Forget that changes cost money.
• Make a consistent policy of encouraging change while insisting that it be worthwhile.	• Reward the ineffective.
• Encourage customers and suppliers to participate in the same system.	• Let a product be changed into a new configuration: develop a new product instead.

PEOPLE ARE PROUD TO WORK THERE.

Do:	Do Not:
• Educate management on how to communicate with people.	• Be inconsistent in personnel policies.
• Establish benefit programs that are practical and meet the needs of the employees.	• Discipline workers publicly.
• Establish formal employee communication and complaint systems through Systems Integrity.	• Have layoffs in order to handle short economic swings.
• Include proud things in the corporate advertising.	• Have different levels of employees such as "hourly" and "salary." Treat all the same way.

"This is an awesome list of things to do, Cynthia," said Foster. "And each one of these has a list under it that needs to be developed."

"How are we going to keep all this in our heads?" asked Victor.

"There are several common threads," said Phil. "If we think of them, the specifics will fit right in. We don't need to create a thick rule book in order to make it come about."

"What threads are you talking about, Phil?" asked Pearl.

"Consistency and Systems Integrity are two of them, and

education is the other I was thinking about," replied Phil. "There are many advantages of predictability, and I think that is what being consistent brings about."

"And you think the Systems Integrity Department is going to be the key to all this?" asked Victor.

"Not the department, although it would provide active support. I was thinking more of the concept of Systems Integrity, that we could depend on this system being something we could use to keep our management actions on the track," replied Phil, getting up to walk around.

"Actually education would be the primary key. Everyone would have to have a clear understanding of the objectives so we could continue to meet them forever."

"Whenever management does anything successful, or solves a complex situation, it always seems to forget the whole thing and go on to something else," said Pearl. "That is just a natural way of operating. As a result the situation repeats itself in a little while."

"That's the business of work being a process," I said. "If the organization operates by treating individual situations one at a time, then there never is a pattern—no consistency, no way to have a built-in, predictable integrity. That way the body is always susceptible to becoming ill—or at least not being well."

Foster waved his hand.

"This all is getting quite beyond me. I have enough trouble explaining to our people that they ought to sell things for more than they cost, and that the stores should be clean. They would be sound asleep by the time I got halfway through that list of items. We are going to have to have a concept and implementation process that is simpler than this."

He pushed his notepad away and laid his glasses on the table.

"Let's make a rule that we can't use anything I can't explain in five minutes. The test would be that the people I explained it to would have to be able to prove they understood it."

Pearl and Victor exchanged glances. They had never been

comfortable with Foster. They just didn't understand that he was as modern as anyone; he just put everything into an "old shoe" format. He liked to break management concepts down to their basics, but he was anything but slow.

"A few years ago," continued Foster, "we decided to set up a new control system so we would know just what we had in each store at any given moment. By using a key number for each product sold in the store and putting that number in the computer as part of the sales transaction, we had a real-time inventory status. Then we cut our major suppliers in on the results so they could send in material at just the right time."

"That sounds like a great program, Foster," I said. "It should have cut inventory cost a great deal."

"Actually it did do that. However it also made it so we had a hard time shutting anything off and ordering new products. The salespeople, and the buyers, if you can imagine, hated it. The customers became uneasy because we didn't have piles of products. We had just what we needed. They thought we were going out of business.

"And then the harshest realization came when it dawned on us that there wasn't anything to have sales with. What good is a department store without sales?

"So we essentially killed the whole system. It would have been very useful and profitable."

He leaned forward and jabbed the air with his finger for emphasis.

"When you decide to change a culture, you'd better be sure you know exactly what is getting changed. We did not do even a reasonable job of explaining it to our employees, suppliers, or customers. That list includes just about everyone involved in the business. Obviously there can be no success, regardless of the soundness of the concept, if there is no understanding. We blew a marvelous opportunity, and it was primarily my fault that we did so."

"How was it your fault?" asked Cynthia. "Certainly top management bears the final responsibility. We all know that, but how can it really be your personal fault?"

"Because I personally limited the education part of the

change. I thought that we could explain it to the managers and then they would pass it on until all employees heard about it from the person they contacted most often. I even made a few speeches about that being the best way to keep people up to speed."

Foster shook his head and put his glasses back on.

"It just seemed to me that the middle managers and supervisors should be responsible for keeping their people informed. Unfortunately it didn't work out. We are going to try again, but we have hired a firm to do the teaching."

"I think you were right originally, Foster," said Victor. "The only missing ingredient was giving the management people some easy to teach material. If they had had videos and workbooks to use, they would have been able to do it themselves."

Pearl liked that idea.

"Then we could do our own continuous education program. People learn better when the instructor is someone who can affect their lives."

"They take it seriously, or more seriously," I said. "I have been through that experience. The quality improvement process has been run that way. Management went to school and then used material provided by the school in order to teach the employees. It has worked out very well. At least we all understand the subject in the same way."

"Quality has had a dramatic improvement, too," said Cynthia. "We really are learning how to get things done right the first time, at least in the areas where management has worked at it."

"I know that our division has not moved as quickly as I would like," said Pearl. "There is a built-in resistance to change in Manufacturing, unless that change is in technology. Then everybody leaps at it. We have a bunch of robots that didn't work out and never will, to prove that point."

"We have had a lot of improvement in Insurance," said Victor. "There was no previous system of quality, so people have been happy to have something to latch on to. They have responded very well to the prepared education program and are actually operating the way it was taught.

"However senior managers in my operation, and I think in Pearl's also," he glanced at Pearl who nodded in confirmation, "have not gotten into it as much as they should. It just takes them time to realize the value of any improvement they didn't create."

"Well, we are talking about a big change and one that has to continue to grow for years," Phil noted. "We can't have it hung up by personality problems. We are going to have to grow our own executives and teach them the principles of successful operation."

"By George, I think you've got it," said Foster. "We could set up a continuing education school for Masters. We could hire a consulting firm to help develop the material, teach our teachers, and then keep an eye on us. That way it would be a Masters' operation, but it would be viewed objectively."

"How long would it take to educate people on the principles of ESO? What do you think, Cynthia?" I asked.

"If we are talking senior managers, I would say five or six weeks, probably spaced out over three months. Then they would have to have something on a regular basis in order to keep up with what is happening."

"Then their subordinates would need instruction in order to understand what the boss was talking about," said Victor. "That would have to be continuing also."

"But it would be videos and workbooks, don't you think?" asked Pearl. "Then we can reach everyone on a continual basis."

"Certainly," said Cynthia. "We could reach everyone on a continual basis. And just doing that would be a big step in helping people have pride in their company and work. One of the major problems we have is that people think the corporation does not care about their future."

"Well," I said, "we seem to have solved the delivery system. The problem now is learning what to deliver, and how to keep it percolating forever. That is not an easy task. Many companies have had similar efforts, only to find that they were not enough."

"True," said Foster. "But the ones I am thinking of didn't aim their educational activities at the overall management concepts of the company. They were concentrating on implementing the policies and practices that had been developed. And even so, when the market and world economy did turn on them, they were able to recover quickly because of the confidence they had built into the management team."

"Sometimes management teams get so confident they doze off," said Victor. "How would we prevent that? I know people who are so convinced that their company has the ideal culture that they can't stand to learn from anyone else."

"Survivors' training," said Phil.

"Every day is a new day," I said.

"Sleep with one eye open," offered Pearl.

"I like 'never close both eyes' better," said Victor.

"Agreed," replied Pearl.

"So we are going into the 'never-close-both-eyes' school of management education. We could learn a lot from the military basic training. I guess that is what we are trying to design, a basic training for managers that makes them ever alert and gives them the tools to defend themselves while attacking enemy territory," I stated.

Everyone sat silently for a moment as we began to absorb all this. It was becoming clearer that there was a great deal more to establishing a specific culture than having some clear concepts. "Eternally Successful Organization" has a much broader and deeper meaning than we had realized. No wonder the little committee that wouldn't could not deal with it. I must apologize to them, I thought.

"Well we can't dress people up in fatigues and run them up and down the hills, but we can put them all through the wellness center, and we can insist that they apply that same sort of discipline to their professional work," Pearl noted.

"And we can provide the tools, resources, and direction to support the educational side of things. Along with that, the management evaluation program will have to be revised in order to deal with real life," said Victor.

"That will be the biggest change of all," I said. "I doubt that there are many honest evaluations done at the managerial level in any company.

"Okay. We have a basic strategy, and we all recognize the need to accomplish it. Cynthia will coordinate for us, Foster and I will explain it to the Board. We don't need its approval, but the members will be pleased to learn that we are working on such an advanced approach."

"How will we select the consultants to help us put this together?" asked Victor.

"I think we should let Cynthia recommend two firms, and then all of us will interview them. I would like someone that approaches the task in the same way the Quality College did. We need to get this done right away," I replied.

"Don't you have a senior management meeting coming up soon?" Foster asked.

"September at Greenbrier. Have you been reading my mind, Foster," I said. "We can lay out the concept and get everyone to agree on it."

"I think we are going to have to help the senior people discover this strategy, chief," said Phil. "I was going to suggest that we restructure our agenda to turn it into a corrective action session."

"How does that work?" I asked.

"We have a guest speaker who lays out the thought that we can control our own destiny. Then we break the attendees into groups to come up with what they see as the biggest problems in the corporation; then we pick the top six or eight of these and ask them to come up with a solution.

"My guess is that they will pick the very problems we have been concerned about. If they have better ones, then we can use them to reshape. But I think it is essential that we make them a real part of the strategy we implement."

"Who all will be there?" asked Cynthia.

"It will be much the same as three years ago," said Phil.

"The top three levels of management and their spouses, plus the members of the Board who can make it. About 110 in all, of which 55 will be in the strategy meetings. Most of the work has to be done in the mornings; they will be expecting some recreation in the afternoons."

"As the golf tournament chairperson, I can assure you that they will plan on getting out at one o'clock to begin teeing off. The tennis players will be following the same path," said Victor.

"We will have plenty of time," said Pearl. "Speeches and your challenge on Tuesday morning, then divide into teams for a couple of hours work. Then Wednesday morning the teams can meet for a couple of hours by themselves and reconvene with the whole group to agree on what we will call the biggest problems; Thursday morning will produce their recommended solutions. Then we can cover the basic strategy needed in order to implement those solutions."

"Sounds like a winner to me," I said. "Phil is that your basic approach?"

"We are all on the same frequency. I have you down to say something at the formal dinner on Wednesday evening. You could put the seal on it at that time, if you wish."

"Done," I agreed. "Thank you all for participating. This will turn out to be a memorable day for Masters and for its future."

13

The Greenbrier Meeting

Phil was cool and composed as we arrived in West Virginia, but I was nervous. It took a younger body to keep its head when all about him were losing theirs. I hadn't gotten around to blaming it all on him, but Kipling sure knew what he was talking about when he wrote the poem, *If.*

However seeing the familiar white building bathed in the green of countless mountain trees calmed me. It is somewhat like going back in time; nothing seems to change here. As the bellhop trundled us to our rooms, I began to think that perhaps the week wouldn't be a complete disaster. My wife, Ellen, had completely ignored my daydreaming and was not too surprised when I cheerfully suggested that we had time for nine holes prior to having dinner at the golf club.

We had been coming to the Greenbrier for many years on a regular basis. Actually the purpose of those visits was to have an annual physical at the clinic. But it was a pleasant experience since they required a person's body only in the morning. That left the afternoon for eating, golfing, and walking through the hills. I had always left refreshed, if a little humbled by the medical probing and pushing.

As Ellen and I walked to the golf club, we met Phil and our guest speaker, Paul Christman, who had the same idea. We signed for lockers, golf carts, greens fees, and a few extra balls. We found our bags already mounted on the carts and, being above practicing, moved directly to the first tee of the Old White course. Ellen waited as we all tried to ignore the stream passing in front of the tee. Her tee was on the other side.

"If you all would support the Equal Rights Amendment," said Ellen, "you could carry your ball over to the red tee with me. Then the water wouldn't be a problem."

"The golf ball industry would collapse in a week Ellen," said Paul. "There would be economic devastation throughout the land. It's better this way."

We finished our nine holes just a little before six and stopped on the veranda of the golf club for a drink. We were supposed to gather for an informal buffet dinner in the club dining room at seven. We decided to just sit there and wait for seven o'clock. There are a lot worse things to be forced into.

"It is an interesting world," said Paul. "My great-great-grandfather worked on a farm 80 miles from here, as a slave."

"And here you are getting paid to sit around and be waited on," I said. "My ancestors, I'm not certain how many *greats* are involved, were shipped to Australia as convicts and worked their way over here somehow."

"My family has only been in this country for two generations," said Ellen. "And we came by ocean liner, first class, I might add. It is a lot better way to get here."

"I'm not really sure where we came from," said Phil. "I grew up in steel country. The parents of most of my friends couldn't speak English. But my family had been around long enough to have lost track of the past."

"We have been helping some companies dig up their histories and publicize them so the employees will know what went on before," said Paul. "It is useful in helping create pride in the company, and it also keeps them on the track by showing them where they have been."

"Is anyone ever tempted to give history a little nudge?" Ellen asked. "I mean do they ever change the founder from a money-grubbing tyrant into a visionary who loved the entire human race?"

"We get hints in that direction, Ellen," he replied. "But if we stick to the facts, and add a little sentiment along the way, then it usually comes out favorable. Actually, in the past, just as today, it was not easy to found a company if you were irascible and untrustworthy. It took a lot of cooperation to get something up and running. They were very determined people."

"As you know, Paul, we have been working on a strategy for making our company eternally successful. Were you able to get briefed on what we plan to do tomorrow?" I asked.

"Right up to date. Phil has kept in touch with me, and I am going to aim my remarks in that direction. The corrective action groups are a good idea, I think. I have used that technique several times, and it always produces very useful information."

"Is this when the audience is divided into small groups and goes off to work out a list of the company's biggest problems?" asked Ellen.

"Right," answered Phil. "Then they come back and list the ones they came up with, and we make a selection of about five or six from all those put forth. Each group gets one of them and goes back to work up what it thinks would be a good solution. The idea is to let everyone have an input into the future strategy of the company."

She turned toward Paul.

"Do companies come up with the same list?" she asked.

Paul smiled.

"I'm not going to tell you too much; you might go into competition with me. There are too many of us as it is. But the lists I have seen are remarkably similar. Companies have different products and markets, but they all have people. People have certain basic requirements when they are together in an organization, whether it is a combat team or a church choir. They worry about those things which usually have to do with communications, management direction, recognition, and the future.

"Then there are operating problems associated with the business itself, which brings up finances, resources, authority, and such."

This was interesting to me. Could it be that we were not the only company in the world trying to solve an enormous problem concerning the future?

"We are not alone then?" I asked.

"Not alone, but way ahead," Paul replied. "Many managements are sitting around contemplating rather than trying to do something about it. They will never catch up with Masters as long as you keep working to formalize success."

"'Formalize success,'" said Phil. "You have a way with phrases. That is exactly what we are trying to do."

"Well the wellness concept is a perfect analogy to use in explaining it to people. And I like your idea of having all the key people go through a center in order to really get the feel of the concept."

"It was your idea. I stole it from an article you wrote."

Paul shook his head.

"I am really slipping. I forget sometimes what I have written and haven't. I write myself notes continually only to find that I have already done what is on the note when I run across it somewhere."

"While we can all remember that much, we'd better be thinking about the buffet. The folks will be arriving," I said.

We all moved into the building and out onto the front veranda where a dozen Masters people had gathered. We soon lost ourselves in conversation.

The next morning we all gathered in the ballroom area, which had been set up in a conference format. Spouses were invited to attend the first two hours if they wished, and many had taken the invitation to heart. Eleanor Landry, the marketing director of Insurance, brought her husband, Jim, over to meet me. Jim was a vice president of a Fortune 500 company and had adjusted his vacation so he could join Eleanor at this meeting.

"We go to each other's corporate strategy sessions," said

Jim. "I enjoy playing 'spouse' and am only here this morning because she dragged me out of bed. I plan to slip off to the baths as soon as it is decent."

"I wanted him to hear Paul Christman," said Eleanor. "Jim still thinks the world is as they explained it when he went to graduate school."

"Well, I'm glad you both are here. Where do you have your strategy meetings, Jim? Do you do it every year?" I asked.

"We do it irregularly, George," he replied. "But every three or four years someone will think it is a good idea and we scramble around to set something up. As you know, if you want to use a place like this, it is necessary to give them some notice. So we are planning on being at The Breakers in Palm Beach next February. The subject will be quality."

"That makes it easy to get top speakers. No one turns down Palm Beach in February," I noted.

"We were hoping that we could get you to come talk to us. I will call your office about it, but I know the old man would really be delighted if you could work us in."

I mumbled something. They went off to their seats, I took mine, and Phil called the meeting to order—exactly on time.

"Welcome," said Phil. "All of you look comfortable and well fed. I am pleased to see that we have so many spouses joining us this morning. We are going to have an interesting time.

"Before we begin the program, there are a few housekeeping announcements, but instead of making them we have pinned them to the board in the back of the room. Please take a long look at break time.

"Our chairperson is with us this morning and will be saying a few words at the dinner Wednesday evening; we also are privileged to have all the members of our Board. I hope each of you will take a moment to welcome them. Our format for the week will concern itself with strategy. Not the kind you do on weekend seminars, but real-life "what are we going to do now" strategy. The future has always been difficult to handle, but now it is really a challenge that requires a broad input. We have to put all our heads together if we are going to keep Masters eternally successful.

"And that is the theme of this strategy session: The Eternally Successful Organization. Our guest speaker, Paul Christman, will discuss the philosophy of ESO. As you know, he comes to us with a depth of experience in practical management, having been CEO of a company he founded, an author, and a professor.

"After Paul's talk we will break into groups of eight. Your room assignment is on the corner of your name badge. There is a little star beside the name of the team leader. Each team will have two hours this morning, and the first hour tomorrow morning, to come up with a list of what you see as the biggest problems Masters has, both currently and in the future.

"We will condense that list to eight items and ask each team to propose a solution to one of them. That result will be a big part of our future strategy for the company. So don't be shy about the problem lists; you will have to live with the result.

"Dr. Raymond Milligen of the Smithers MBA school will provide us with some guidance on pulling all this together. Ray will also be available to the team leaders and, in fact, had several conferences with them over the past few weeks. So they are well prepared.

"After Paul's comments we will have a period of questions and answers, then a break, and then the teams will go to their rooms. Tomorrow morning teams will meet again in their rooms and we will all come together here at 9 am. And now I have the honor to introduce my friend Paul Christman."

Paul moved to the podium in the midst of polite applause, fastened the lapel microphone to his tie, and smiled at the group. He laid his prepared remarks on the lectern, opened the folder, and then moved over to the center of the stage.

> I am very pleased to be with you today because I believe that it is going to be a memorable one in your personal history, as well as in the history of Masters.
>
> This will be the launching of a formal strategy de-

signed to help the company be perpetually successful. The corrective action sessions you will conduct are going to be a big part of defining and implementing the necessary strategy.

It would be nice if there were just one specific set of actions a management group could take in order to produce success. It would be nice if there were a list of things not to do in order to keep from causing problems. But corporate life is more complex than that.

I have a friend who fancies himself an entrepreneur and has spent a fortune trying to prove it. He has had several businesses shot out from under him. Each time, he selected a product or service he figured everyone was dying to have, and then he made a business plan. The plan showed exactly how the business would progress over the next few years.

He used this plan to bring venture money into the business, and it worked every time because the investors figured something so well thought out can't be anything but successful. He set up the business, gained some customers, and then slowly went down the chute. All the while this went on, he and his advisors met regularly, tracking the business according to the plan. When they used all the money, the business was over.

They diligently measured compliance with the plan and were very happy when it progressed that way. However when all the money was spent, they looked around to discover that they did not have a business. But they felt real good managing the plan without spending too much thought on customers or employees.

Corporate executives usually are too experienced to become trapped into the whirlpool a rigid plan can create. However, executives have concentrated for years on their products, to the exclusion of any other activity. They are busy measuring, sharpening, and honing them in order to attain the maximum in both customer satisfaction and corporate profits. This has been usual in most businesses because that is the part of the operation closest to the customer. It isn't very efficient. It does keep things running, but the company is a day-to-day activity.

To prevent the failure of a company, it is necessary to put things into perspective. The future needs attention. Companies, and industries, die because they did not think of what is yet to come. They did not pay enough attention to their employees and customers. They were interested in their products to the exclusion of everything else.

Every business has products, whether they be bank loans, computer programs, forgings, automobiles, advice, educational programs, or some of the million other possibilities. The products are what everyone talks about, measures, tries to develop more of, and counts in order to calibrate success.

I just spent some time with a government regulatory agency. One of its people commented that the agency does not have a product. All it does is go around and regulate. It doesn't even have a real customer, except, of course, Congress and the American people.

However, the agency does have a product, which is the audit it performs in order to see if the businesses it regulates are sound. It provides a seal of approval, or at least an absence of disapproval, that is valuable to the management of that business.

When I ask executives, such as yourselves, what they work on, I usually hear about the product of their organization. And the description invariably includes many initials and acronyms, which displays a great deal of familiarity and confidence. People working on the same thing can have a long conversation without ever using a proper word. All they need is a verb now and then. I picked up one memo during a visit to your insurance operation last month. Let me read you some of the initials: HID; IIR; DEMAC; C.A.S.H.; VOL; WALPRT. I feel like Professor Higgins.

The reason I am belaboring this obvious point is to let us all understand where our heads lie: they lie in the products of the organization. However, the heart and soul of a corporation do not lie in its products. Rather it rests in the process that produces the output of the organization. The artist has to have a well-run mind and body in order to cause art to appear. It is necessary to provide art that someone will buy, as well as something that is satisfying to the producer.

The product leads the company in most cases, rather than the other way around. The company becomes so familiar with it that it doesn't notice itself growing out of favor. Any corrective action taken is directed at the product: making new ones, remarketing the old one, a new advertising agency, everything for the product. I have a client who persists in putting a few hundred changes a month into a product that is 25 years old and losing market share.

A pattern emerges after a while. You have noticed that many nations never seem to progress. On the ESO grid they would register as comatose. They have a long history of not getting anywhere. A large segment of the population lives in poverty. The bright young people leave as soon as they can for places providing more opportunity and appreciation. Yet it is not for lack of effort. There are many cases where groups of the best people, with the most talent and influence, band together with everyone's support in order to find a solution to the problem.

They usually come up with an economic plan where business will be invited in to start activities that will provide jobs. Jobs, it is believed, will take people out of poverty and let them have the opportunity to build a life. Special tax arrangements, and perhaps direct funding, are made available to the businesses, and they do come in. Everyone is very enthusiastic.

Then what happens? It doesn't take long before the people are being difficult. They realize that all the jobs imported to their land appear to be low-level. The management has been brought in for the most part. The young people of the nation leave for brighter shores as soon as they get the chance. Nothing improves again. The companies eventually tire of it and trickle off.

The well-intentioned officials have not realized that the problem is in the process, and that working at the wrong end of it creates nothing of lasting worth. They have not thought about the infrastructure that provides education, facilities, financial backing, encouragement, rewards, and such that help people build a life. Just providing low-level jobs is not much more than a welfare program that makes everyone feel less guilty about it all.

Let me repeat: "The problem is in the process." Having said that and having watched you stare vacantly back while listening to me say it, I think it is about time I got around to my point. It is something you are aware of, but you have never been in a situation where you could do much about it. Business organizations usually do not recognize that the product is the result of the culture of the organization, not the other way around. Other organizations do realize it and work that way.

• Athletic teams concentrate on attitude, pride, and basics. Teams that play well usually have the highest attendance of those who advertise the best. Performance is the product.

• Higher education organizations create an environment in which learning is a desirable venture. They create group efforts for people to join, and they coat their graduates with tradition and reputation. They don't sell education. They provide an experience and something to live by after the specific knowledge is outmoded.

Cultures can be created once a basic set of principles has been defined and understood. The principles involved in our effort this week, and, I hope, into the future, are built around what we call the characteristics of an eternally successful organization. These are the culture basics that management has to cause to happen. The result is a company that performs well in the areas of finance, products, and other business activities. The process is in hand and operating properly at all times.

Imagine how wonderful it would be to manage a company where people routinely did what they had agreed to do, where growth was steady and profitable, where customers' needs were anticipated, where change was encouraged and managed, and where the people were proud to work there.

It would be possible for an executive to think something out, discuss its accomplishment with others, develop an implementation plan, and execute the entire event with efficiency and no hassle. Satisfied customers, satisfied employees, satisfied self.

An impractical dream? Just another seminar subject? Something we might get around to one day after all the real problems are solved?

Not so.

Making it happen is well within our grasp. Keeping it happening is a matter of placing priorities and granting permission—eternal vigilance and eternal dedication.

Let's take these characteristics one at a time. Then we can have a discussion period before you go off to the breakout rooms.

First, "People routinely do things right the first time."

A lot of work has been going on in this area. If there were any skeptics about its value, I think some numbers Phil gave me this morning will cause them to rethink things. About a year ago when the quality improvement process was formally begun, the comptroller's office, assisted by the consultant, and the Quality Improvement Team, set up a procedure for calculating the price of nonconformance. Since that time, it has been tracked faithfully.

A great deal of that expense relates directly to people

not doing things right the first time, for a variety of reasons. At any rate, let me unveil these charts.

You can see that insurance had an annual PONC rate of $52 million, or $1 million a week. That rate has dropped by one-third in the first year.

The biggest reduction has been in reprocessing, which Cynthia tells me is primarily due to improved communication between supervisors and the employees, plus the application prevention tools learned in the quality education system classes. Field Service is beginning to reduce its waste expenses also.

Manufacturing has not been involved as long, but its improvement is on the same path. It also has had a one-third reduction in PONC. Most of that is from rework and scrap elimination.

The stimulating part is that Manufacturing projects will reduce excess inventory to zero in a year. Manufacturing just does not have to overorder any more. Warranty and Field Service will follow the same path.

So far we are talking about an annual reduction of $47 million, all due to reeducating management and employees to understand quality in the same way. When we learn to work that way routinely, we will take a great deal of cost and hassle out of the company. And we will build a foundation within the company that lets us pay attention to the positive factors instead of just fighting to keep up.

One thing has been made clear to us: Quality is a choice management can make.

Second, "Growth is profitable and steady."

Growing is something a company has to do if it is to be around forever. Humans keep growing throughout their lives; it is a necessary part of coping and overcoming. People don't keep getting taller, or necessarily heavier, but they do have to continue to develop in order to be successful in all aspects of life. Growth is part of wellness.

Organizations tend to look at growth as additions to

the asset side of the ledger only. Therefore they get into acquisitions as the primary source of making this happen. If they achieve a fit of culture, products, and income, this often works out well.

However the real basis for growth often comes from knowing how to use better what is already around. Mental development in the individual is what brings success and recognition. The same applies in organizations. Producing what the world wants and growing profitably because of it is the sure way of staying successful. Knowing how to do that comes from creating a corporate and personal culture that permits it to happen. Wellness is no accident.

Third, "Customer needs are anticipated."

When new products and services appear as needed, and customer desire is met even before customers are aware that it is important to them, then we are applying the proper concentration to this matter.

This does not mean being constantly exposed by guessing about customer needs. Rather it requires continual awareness, research, and internal cooperation, plus a positive relationship with the customer. Development is done deliberately and innovatively.

Fourth, "Change is planned and managed."

Change is our friend if we control it properly, and since it will happen anyway, we need to learn how to manage it. Systems Integrity is the method Masters has developed to deal with change and to assure conformance to existing requirements.

Fifth, "People are proud to work there."

Communication, example, and participation are the three legs of the platform for pride. Members of any organization want to be proud of it. Implementing that intent takes specific action on the part of management. Why some companies choose to be rude and insensitive to their employees is something I have never understood.

Just as quality is not left in the hands of the quality

professionals, so the responsibility for pride should not be dumped on Human Resources. In both cases the subjects have to be tended and managed, but there are many causes of problems in both areas that cannot be handled by techniques and procedures.

Senior management bears a large part of the responsibility in creating and environment in which pride is encouraged to blossom.

We have some time before the break and your trip to the conference rooms. We can talk about whatever you would like to talk about. I will repeat your question so everyone will be able to hear it.

QUESTION: This sounds like the way to go, Paul, and I am interested in learning more about it. One thing can't be overlooked, and that is cost. How much is it going to cost us to make a massive culture change like this and then maintain it over the years? Will we have to add a couple of percent to our pretax earnings?

ANSWER: It should cost us a lot less to operate this way. Let me give you two for-instances: turnover in insurance sales personnel costs us $9 million every year. That is just replacement and training of new people. We don't know how much business is lost in the meantime. The primary reason people give for leaving Masters is that they think their input of ideas is not expected or appreciated. That is something we should be able to change. Second, we have had an annualized price of nonconformance reduction of around $47 million. That cost us about $500,000 so far. This is what we paid for the educational and consulting program with the firm helping us. When we are completely set up and self-operating in the quality improvement area, plus having the consultants keep our educational process up to date, we will have spent a total of $1,300,000. That represents fewer than three days of PONC at our start-off rate. To save you all the math, we were spending about $580,000 a day doing things wrong. Our current rate is at $400,000 daily. It should get to $150,000 by the end of next year. Prevention pays off and pays its own way. Yes sir?

QUESTION: Are we going to have educational support to help our people absorb all this?

ANSWER: That is up to you. The characteristics I just outlined are not an operating plan. They are a description of a corporate environment that will keep a company well. Making that happen is another process. I think you will have a better feeling about what has to happen after the sessions today. But I think the senior management can have whatever it wants in order to do what it wants.

Phil stepped to the lectern.

"I hate to interrupt, but if we are going to keep on schedule, we will need to get on to the next event. Let's thank Paul for his comments this morning."

After the applause he reminded them to check the bulletin boards, and the group moved into the hall for coffee and conversation.

"Good job, Paul," I said, shaking his hand. "We are off to a good beginning. I hope they take it seriously."

"Oh they do," said Paul. "You couldn't see their faces, but I could. They will work hard on the problem and solution lists."

"Coffee?" asked Phil.

"Thank you," said Paul.

"I'd like to know what problems will wind up on the main list," I said.

"A couple always appear," said Paul. "Management doesn't listen, objectives are unrealistic, resources are not distributed where they are needed, communication is erratic—those are a few."

"I'd like to see us get more specific than that," said Phil.

"It takes a couple of rounds," replied Paul. "But they will get specific once they see you two are serious."

He put down his cup.

"You see, they know that the only ones who can actually change things are you two, and even Phil has to have your agreement, George, in order to make anything happen. Companies are dictatorships regardless of all the talk about consensus and participative management. So they will be watching very closely to see what the reaction and action is."

"I guess I'd better get to work on my speech for tomorrow evening," I mumbled.

14

The "Biggest Problem" Meetings

Harrison Room
Group 3:
    Eleanor Landry, team leader
    Jack Rudolph (Finance)
    Peter Miller (Purchasing)
    Louis O'Conner (Manufacturing)
    LeRoy Carrell (Group Exec)
    Walter John (Human Resources)
    Will Anderson (Sales)

ELEANOR: Now I don't want any trouble with you people. I have the power to have you removed from the golf and tennis tournaments if you are not cooperative.

PETER: Don't worry about us, Eleanor. We are all as docile as lambs. Just tell us what you want us to write down, and it is as good as done.

LEROY: Is there coffee in here? I got to talking out in the hall and missed it.

ELEANOR: Over there in the corner, LeRoy.

LEROY: Thanks, chief. Can I get you some?

ELEANOR: Please, just black.

WALTER: I am surprised that we didn't know anything about this biggest problem list business. We could have done some preparation before coming here.

LOUIS: I guess they figured we could remember the things that are bugging us. I have a list embedded on my heart. Right here, under my Greenbrier logo.

ELEANOR: If we are all settled, we need to agree on some ground rules. What we are asked to do is make a simple list of what we see as the most significant problems facing the company and, of course, the management of the company. The items have to be specific. We can't say "people," or "communications," or general items like that.

WALTER: How many can we have?

ELEANOR: All we want, although I would suspect they would like to wind up with 8 to 10 after everyone has had input. It would be hard to manage a list much bigger.

LOUIS: Can we be general enough to say something like: Senior management doesn't listen very well?

JACK: I agree on that one, but don't forget we are supposed to be senior management.

LOUIS: What did you say? I didn't hear you.

JACK: Point.

ELEANOR: I would suggest that we do this in two ways. First let's see if anyone has a really burning issue that he or she considers a "biggest problem"; then after that we can brainstorm until we have a list that is suitable for trimming. Anyone have trouble with that approach?

PETER: I would like to bring up a "burning issue."

ELEANOR: Burn away.

PETER: The employees of the company do not believe that they, as individuals, are integral components of the organization.

LOUIS: You mean they don't feel like they belong?

PETER: A little deeper than that, but that is the idea.

WALTER: Most of them seem happy. We get very few complaints.

LOUIS: We treat them better than any other company they could go to work for.

PETER: All true. I guess I am talking about ownership, and I don't mean stocks.

ELEANOR: A sense of stability? Okay, what other burning issue?

JACK: Information systems are just not up to what we need. We should be able to communicate throughout the corporation with a common database from terminals in our offices.

LOUIS: There is some of that now; I can watch a lot of things from my desk terminal.

JACK: I appreciate that, but there is a whole possible world of communications that we haven't even touched, and it is growing every day. We are behind, if the future is what we are worried about.

ELEANOR: Information systems as the basis for communication in the corporation. Okay, what other burning issues?

LEROY: I worry about our customer research and using that to keep ahead of the competition on products. We missed two breakouts in insurance in the last year, and we have been criticized for having obsolete manufactured products.

LOUIS: Much of that has been an inability to get management support for the capital items needed.

LEROY: True, and that lack of support comes from the absence of data to show that it is needed. That data comes from research.

ELEANOR: In this kind of research it is difficult to come up with the kind of hard facts the capital committee wants. We need some other way of looking at it. How about "require a system of customer need research that produces trustworthy data"?

LEROY: Sold.

ELEANOR: We have three burning issues, any more?

LOUIS: We have made a lot of progress in quality, but it has been the easy stuff so far. I would not want it to be a forgotten item on this problem list.

ELEANOR: Good point, it will be on the list. Many people do not need much success to take something off the problem list. Let's go on to the brainstorming items. I am getting anxious to attack that buffet down at the golf club.

The next morning Phil rose to address the group. A screen and projector had been set up earlier, and he had carefully tried them out.

"I don't need our biggest problem to be a president who can't show a chart straight," he said. "That sort of thing detracts from the meeting and gives a bad impression. If I had my way, we would never use anything that could go wrong."

Calling the meeting to order, he got right on with it.

"Each of the groups handed a problem list in right on time, and the team leaders sat with me to help meld them all together. I want to congratulate all of you on the thoughtful-

ness with which you approached this task. It is apparent from
the items listed that you know the company well and also are
well informed on the business and real worlds.

"We combined some problems, and omitted a few that can
be addressed in other ways. You will receive a report a little
later that will include every item mentioned. However at this
time we will limit ourselves to eight problems that the group
thought were the most significant for us to get involved with
at this time.

He laid a foil on the chart.

"I thought we would take them one at a time. Each foil will
contain the problem and the task team it has been assigned
to. The teams will report to us tomorrow concerning their
recommendations for action. Please contact members of
those teams if you have any input to give. We are going to
need a lot of ideas. This is quite a list we have.

"I will start through them in no particular order."

He flipped the switch.

The chart read: "The quality improvement effort is not
embedded into the company, its systems, its suppliers, its customers, and its people." (Team 1 assigned.)

"I am not going to comment on them", said Phil. "I'll go
through them and pause with each one. If anyone has any
questions or comments, just speak up. Otherwise we will proceed to look at them all and then break up into teams. A list
of all eight problems and the teams assigned is on the table in
the back of the room. Pick one up on your way out this morning.

"If there are no questions, here is the next one."

"The internal information system program is too narrow
to permit true business communications throughout the company." (Team 2 assigned.)

"The performance evaluation program and the personnel
compensation system do not reward merit or encourage innovation." (Team 3 assigned.)

"Senior management is not reasonably available to participate on a regular basis and is not actively listening." (Team 4
assigned.)

"Employees, while loyal to the company, do not feel personal ownership to the point necessary for a massive improvement effort." (Team 5 assigned.)

"We do not have a proven way of knowing what customers are thinking about or needing." (Team 6 assigned.)

"The margins are beginning to become smaller each year, and the cash flow is a little less, proportionally, than it was. This has tended to delay projects and reduce options." (Team 7 assigned.)

"The base of the company is too narrow, having two divisions, in two businesses that do not feed each other." (Team 8 assigned.)

"I think that is an awesome list," said Phil. "George and I will be here, in this room, while you all return to your tasks. If anyone wants our comment or input on anything, just let us know. We will be actively participating and listening."

He smiled, as did everyone else, and off they went. I was pleased with the list and thought something might happen as a result of it. But then, I have been wrong before.

"I haven't been watching the margins closely, Phil," I said. "But I hadn't had any feeling that they were slipping. Are they?"

He shook his head.

"No. I think the item is referring to the margins not getting any bigger. We have been looking at reducing expenses and are about ready to begin a quiet crunch along those lines. It is possible to reduce about 5 percent through attrition of people, but I would like us to combine facilities and other areas to see if they couldn't drop 15 percent."

"That would be a big venture," I said. "How long would it take?"

"Probably three years. If we can figure how to grow without spending more money, it will take care of itself."

Paul came into the room.

"I have been sitting in on one of the task teams. They are really taking this seriously," he said. "I hear a lot of 'back to the basics' type of conversation in the halls."

"Most of them are too young to know what the basics really

are," I noted. "It would be like going back to boot camp. However it isn't a bad idea. At least everyone could understand the business."

"There is another good point coming out of this," said Paul. "It combines the problem about the information system and top management not being participative enough."

Phil and I both leaned forward, unconsciously.

"Top managers have always been traditionally dependent on lower managers to keep them informed and to provide specific knowledge about specific things. However if the data system is structured properly, they can have as much information as anyone else, right on their own desktop computer."

"We have some now," Phil said.

"But you never look at it to help make decisions. Both of you, like your counterparts everywhere, call a group together, examine the data, and then make a decision. Right?" He smiled at us.

"We agree," I said. "But what's the message?"

"The message is that top managers are forever setting up systems and programs to make everything run more efficiently, but they don't use them personally, and they don't participate with others that do use them. Therefore the people who actually control the place on a complete basis are out of the loop."

Phil stood up and began to move about.

"So all the strategy, consensus management, and other things we go through don't necessarily mean much?"

"Well they mean something," said Paul. "But the fact of real life is that in most companies the chairperson and president make it all up as they go along. And, for the most part, it works out rather well. At least on a short-term basis."

"And the value of consensus?" I asked.

"People like to be involved and know what is going on," he replied. "But they have their own problems and really can't look at the whole world of the company when they are held responsible for one operation."

"We can delegate operations, but not leadership?" I asked.

"Is that what you are saying? I'm not certain I agree with that."

"Well nothing is absolute in every respect, as you know, but essentially that it the way it works out. Let's take a look at these eight biggest problems that were laid out this morning.

"First is that the Quality Improvement Process is not 'embedded' in the company and all those who touch it."

"That is true," said Phil, "but a great deal has been accomplished and more is on the way. We have great teams working on it all across the corporation. Everyone is very enthusiastic."

"Right," said Paul. "But the word they chose is 'embedded.' That means something that is set firmly in place with no expectation that it will ever be moved. Setting up Systems Integrity shows clearly that both of you are serious about quality and intend to see that it is embedded. You have it deep in your mind that quality can be caused and that routine problem prevention is where the company needs to be. Because of this concern and attention on the part of the very tip of the pyramid, which is you two, quality is getting there."

"Then why did they make it the first problem?" I asked.

"There really weren't any problem priorities set, George," said Phil. "I just stacked them that way. However to be honest about it, I did put quality first because I wanted Team 1 to deal with it. However, it really is a lot further ahead than they might think, they just don't have as much information about what is happening. A report will come out later this month that will provide a great deal of encouragement.

"When everyone had to go to class, including you two, and bad doers had their knuckles spanked for not following the requirements, and customer problems were taken seriously, then the thought leaders began to see that this was something worth doing.

"The Quality Improvement Process is a good example of what I am talking about."

Phil came over and sat, Paul pulled up a chair next to me, and we all leaned into the circle.

"You deliberately changed the culture of the company by

replacing the old attitude of 'close enough is good enough' with 'do it right the first time.' There were no policies or programs describing the old policy, but it was real. The management felt that way and so did everyone else.

"Changing it required education and demonstration. Given another year or two, it would take a similar process to drive it out and back to the old way."

I was beginning to get a slight tummy ache.

"Are you saying that programs work only if they reflect accurately the behavior and thought processes of the headquarters? That must be why the equal opportunity efforts don't work some places and are no problem in others. It isn't the system or the law; it is the local environment. You can't fool people on these things."

"Precisely," said Paul.

"Let's look at these other problems," said Phil. "The second one says the internal information system doesn't have a broad enough database, and we don't know how to use it properly. Now what could George do differently, or me for that matter?"

Paul nodded.

"Okay, if you really used that data bank, and the network that goes along with it, as a primary source of information for running the company, others would also. That means a great deal more would be required in it. Believe me, it would appear. They want to be on the same frequency as you."

"But I find those computers difficult to operate," I pleaded. I have a hard time understanding the language. Secretly, I don't really like or trust them. I guess I should quit pretending that I do."

"If you want a worldwide network that lets decision making drop a couple of levels and improves internal communication by a factor of 10, then you have to figure something out. There is nothing that says you can't have an operator who brings up the information you want. All you need is a terminal that doesn't even have to have a keyboard. Then on the phone, or in person, you just ask to see what you want. If you get hooked, then there will be no problem."

Paul felt as if he were plowing virgin ground; I could tell. He was also thinking, I'm sure, that we had never thought about these things in this way before. He was correct.

"The third problem is on performance evaluation," read Phil. "I agree that our system leaves a lot to be desired. But so do all the others I have ever seen. Do you know a better one?"

"Not much better," said Paul. "They are all designed to make things convenient for the evaluator, not to help the individual. I do have a few ideas, but they probably are not too original. This is one that a team can actually help on, once it is decided that it is something the company really wants.

"Performance reviews probably do more to make employees antagonistic to their company than any other single item. If you are interested, I will send you an article on it. Actually it is a chapter of a book I was working on but set aside last year. This is the only part of it I liked."

"Can you get involved in writing a book, decide you don't like it, and then just quit?" I asked. "I thought authors loved their work."

"Not after the first three or four books. After that it is more difficult to work up continuous enthusiasm. It takes a couple of years for me to write one," he replied.

"This is one I really don't understand," said Phil. "Senior management is not reasonably available to participate on a regular basis and is not actively listening."

"This is a big company," I said rather snappily. "There is no way I can get to everyone."

"I don't think they expect to see you regularly," noted Paul. "But they want you, and Phil, to know what they are doing. That takes us back to Item 2 about the internal information system. If their summary data were on your screen regularly, they would know it and so would you."

"Employees do not feel ownership," read Phil. "This is a hard one. Some people never belong, or want to. Others will put up with a lot before becoming disappointed. I never understood the difference."

"I'm with you," I said. "I really don't know how to make

people loyal, or even proud. They are probably the same thing, or at least grow in the same womb."

"We'll work on that," said Paul. "But there is an answer, and it revolves around the respect they think the company has or doesn't have for them. I am not really certain how to always show people respect, but I think a lot has been learned about what not to do."

"We could check out some bad examples, like government offices," I said.

"A good example," nodded Paul. "In the same agency you can find herds of people who feel deeply respected and herds of people in open revolt. Same pay scales, same basic work, same very senior management. Different attitude altogether. It is not an easy situation to manage."

Phil was determined to discuss the entire list.

"We do not have a proven way of knowing what customers are thinking about or needing." He thumped the paper. "I really think that this sort of listing is a copout. Some people just want a room service menu of how to keep the customers satisfied."

"This will be another task for which a team will be able to provide a lot of help," said Paul. "Customer research is a never-ending operation, and that group will come up with something very practical and useful with a little encouragement."

"I can remember from my marketing days," said Phil, "that the problem was not finding out what the customers wanted; it was getting someone to do it that way.

"When I was working with a consumer products company, we learned that customers liked our packaging all right, but they were beginning to look for smaller packages, too. Then they could use these when they traveled or went on vacation.

"Do you think I could get anyone interested in those packages? We put together a complete cost program, showing we would get the development money back in 11 months and would have an enormous margin to boot. But Manufacturing killed it; it didn't have the capacity, the department said.

"Management ignored the whole thing. Our competitors

came out with a line of miniatures the next year and shut us out. I was gone by that time."

Paul and I were about to tell of our own experiences along that line when we began to realize that time was running out.

"Let's look at the others," I said. "If I am correct, one was about the margins getting smaller and the last had to do with having only two businesses that do not feed each other."

"Yes," said Phil, "the margin one referred to cashflow and the reduced options it produced."

"Now that also is one for which a team can provide good guidance and action. Right Paul?"

"Right," he said. "There is a clear difference in all these problems. To me the score is top management 4, task teams 4. You all have to tackle quality, information systems, pride, and management availability.

"The teams can be expected to be productive on performance appraisal (you will have to let them know you really want to have honest and useful evaluations), customer research, cash flow, and broadening our base, if that turns out to make sense."

I shook Paul's hand.

"You have been very helpful," I said. "I have to think about this and rewrite my speech for tonight. The teams are breaking up; let's go join them for lunch."

15

The Dinner Speech

"We never have head tables," I told Jack Rudolph. "There is a deep philosophical reason for that, I'm sure. The real reason is that I can't stand to sit there in front of everyone and eat with one view."

"And he likes to get up and move around the room," inserted Ellen. "Head tables cramp his style."

As the servers began to clean the tables, Phil moved to the lectern and introduced the activities chairpersons who distributed the prizes for golf and tennis. I always felt left out when it came time for the awards. I didn't play tennis, and my golf game was neither good nor bad enough to win anything. So I concentrated on my notes.

I didn't want this to be just another short speech. I believed we were on the cusp of something important. It seemed to me that we were near to developing a whole new approach to management, if we could only get the concepts together. I hoped to bring them into the thought pattern.

The athletic prizes were distributed, the tables were cleared, and I was next, ready or not. Phil introduced me, everyone provided polite applause, and I walked to the lectern.

I looked around the room at all those positive friendly faces, and for some reason I recalled the days when I was sitting there and the chairperson came up to make a speech. It brought back the feelings of both hope and fear that such occasions brought forth—hope that perhaps something favorable might be forthcoming and fear that some change might be appearing that would put a bubble in all my career plans.

Now as they all settled down and I spread my notes on the lectern, I determined to remember my beginnings and be useful while remembering my job, which was to be challenging and sometimes difficult. Realizing that I never seemed to get better at making intimate speeches, I took a quiet breath, smiled, and began.

> I am delighted that we are all here together tonight. Our company is doing well, thanks to you, and we look out into a future that is unlike anything that has ever been looked out into.
>
> Frankly, I have been concerned about that future. Specifically, I have been wondering if the management approaches and cultures that have become normal over the years just may not be enough to guarantee success. Business is becoming less forgiving. There are no easy holes to play, and every bad shot can be terminal. In general, management still does things the way they were done years ago. And we continue to teach new managers the same styles. We have traded Bob Cratchet's quill pen for a word processor, but the procedure is still the same.
>
> Masters is not much different from other corporations when it comes to the management strategy. I suspect that many of the problems in the list we developed over the past two days would be applicable to most organizations. One of our consultants even predicted, with considerable accuracy, what much of the list would contain. You did fool him in a couple of cases, which shows a comprehension of the business that is above what is normally anticipated. You are to be congratulated on that.
>
> Our problem with the future does not lie just in a list of things that need to be done to resolve current problems. Knowing this team, we will indeed take effective action against those items. Corrective action has always

been a strong suit of ours. No, the real problem is in what action we actually take to learn how to prevent such situations from ever happening at all. We need to reach a point where sessions like this produce a list of problems that relate only to opportunities for future accomplishments, not to survival alone.

If we think back over our personal careers, both at Masters and other employers, it is quite clear that it is a very rare instance when a problem was so well solved and prevented that it disappeared forever. Often the attempts at correction produced a solution that became a bigger problem than the original one. We opened boxes that contained things of which we had no conception. Electronic assembly contains dozens of these, and the insurance business produces them like mushrooms in a dark forest. They all occurred because we really didn't understand the situation clearly. Causes are more complex in this day.

The significance of this awareness is that we have little time to work on the future if we are continually spending our time rearranging the past.

That may be the most meaningful thing I am going to say this evening: We need to learn how to spend our time and effort working on the future instead of continually rearranging the past.

I think of this as causing corporate wellness. If we take care not to get sick, then we don't need to take the measures necessary to become well again. Wellness is what we are after. At present the only thing we are doing that fits this concept is the Quality Improvement Process. We are learning to prevent problems rather than develop unique actions to solve them. We need to be able to do that throughout the company.

I am going to propose that we begin an educational activity—Not training, education. Some we can do inside; some we would do in conjunction with resources outside the company. We have to find people or organizations who really understand their subjects. All of us have to learn how to prevent problems and at the same time grow the next generation of executives, managers, knowledge workers, and skilled employees.

We have to learn to do things right the first time, to cause and yet control change, to understand how to help the customers in ways they haven't even thought about yet, to grow in a manner that is continually profitable and prepares us for the future, and to help our people be proud to work here at Masters.

The subjects involved would be specific concerning those tasks but also include human relations, communication, ethics, and the concepts and skills of preventing. As part of this we will need to create a performance appraisal system that truly recognizes merit and provides a road map for both those who are reviewed and those who manage that particular process.

I think we should look at our incentive compensation plan and realize that people just think of it as another way of getting their pay in a slow fashion. We need to tie it into profit sharing in a clear manner, and wrap that up in stock purchases. So much of the incentive compensation goes into stock, and the company adds to it. That way we can help people create wealth. This will help them have a closer relationship to the company.

We need to learn how to manage our customer relations so that we don't have ups and downs that require layoffs. There is a lot to be said for consistent employment, and it is a lot less expensive to handle.

We also need to learn how to bring Systems Integrity into the bone marrow of every Masters employee. We have to be able to depend on each other. As part of this, perhaps we should begin calling the people who work here, including ourselves, associates.

[They were actually taking notes about this. I could imagine the projected organization charts rattling around in a few heads. It would take a while for it to dawn on some of them that we were talking culture, not procedures.]

Creating an environment that lets people feel like part of a family establishes a concern for the company's health and welfare that does not exist today. It is the difference between owning and renting. No one cares as much about a rental as about personally owned property.

Creating an environment of continual learning and personal expansion establishes a loyalty that does not exist when people do not have a common language and understanding. It is the difference between participating in the excitement of learning with others or taking lonely TV courses. A college provides a person with an identity; solo courses just provide information.

Creating an environment of openess and availability establishes the opportunity for the science of management to grow and prosper. It is the difference between doing things on purpose and reacting to what is happening. Most management concepts and techniques are directed toward solving problems. We want to learn how to make them not happen.

It is often said that if you aren't making mistakes you aren't trying hard. I think that isn't true. I think we can innovate and execute continually without lurching from semidisaster to real disaster.

So we have a big challenge before us and a wonderful opportunity, not only for Masters but for ourselves as individuals. We are setting out to create the world's first eternally successful profit-making organization.

All those poorly managed fumbling churches and universities that have been around for hundreds of years exist and grow because people want them to exist and grow. Their environment assumes eternity. They manage that environment.

Managerial skills and techniques won't save us; They help, but they are only a part. Our attitude and culture are the key. We need to work at being well, and take it as seriously as we do when we are sick. It needs our full attention.

Thank you.

[The applause was much more than polite. I began to believe that we could really make it happen.]

"It goes without saying," said Sandy, "that we have to pay precise attention to accounting and to financial management. However if we really don't say much about it, then it will go without happening as well as without saying."

"By which you mean," said Phil, "that every policy has to take finance into consideration. We have to plan, budget, and control things very carefully, or all the other efforts will be for naught."

"Right," said Sandy.

"Also," I put in, "we need to have associates to be able to make inputs continually. It is very easy to become complacent and slip away from communicating with them."

"That is the way most companies start having problems with their employees. The old 'nobody listens' routine. Somehow it always happens when success rears its ugly head," said Sandy.

"Well, someone needs to be in charge of it, just like everything else. You know, the consumer product companies, which have hundreds of different products, put someone in charge of each one. They also have a different person in charge of advertising, and they encourage these individual brand managers to try to take the whole market even if that means crawling over another of their own products," Phil said.

"We don't need to get that involved, but we do need to be watchdogs of the policies we are setting up. I think that should be a part of Systems Integrity," I stated.

"I think the brand manager idea would work well with all these characteristics we are concerned about; we can't expect Human Resources to be objective about them. We have to force ourselves to learn prevention and communication," said Sandy.

"I think we're on our way," I said. "It will take forever, but then that is how long we have."

16

Epilogue

Well, it has been seven years now. Phil has been chairperson and CEO for five years. I have been retired all that time but still serve on the Board. This will be my last year, and I am honestly looking forward to it. The company has done well, even though I have become much more interested in grand-children than statistics. Foster goes off the same time I do. He is still CEO of his stores, but I can see that he is losing interest fast.

Masters has been making excellent progress on the ESO project and has changed the culture quite a bit. I haven't been that close to it, but the things we discuss in the Board meetings are different from what they used to be.

Foster and I talked about it one day and decided to ask Phil if we could conduct a status review and do a report card as we did eight years ago. He thought that was an excellent idea and asked Cynthia, now an executive vice president, to set it up. Since the same subject was reviewed routinely at management meetings, we would not be causing extra work.

Cynthia assured me that she would be delighted to do a "then and now" look.

"You are going to be really surprised at what evolved out of that long-ago Audit Committee meeting. We have more scientific ways of measuring and evaluating now, but basically we are following the same approach conceived at that time."

She laid a chart on the overhead projector and turned it on.

REPORT CARD

	Then	*Now*
People do things right routinely.	Progressive Care	Wellness
Growth is steady and profitable.	Intensive Care	Healing
Customer needs are anticipated.	Progressive Care	Healing
Change is planned and managed.	Intensive Care	Wellness
People are proud to work there.	Progressive Care	Healing

"That is a dramatic improvement," I said. "I have noticed over the past five years that a great many recurring problems were not recurring anymore."

"How about the Price of Nonconformance?" asked Foster. "We are a much bigger company now. Has it changed, percentagewise?"

"I have charts on that too, Foster. I knew you would ask. When we first looked at PONC eight years ago, it represented 29.6 percent of Manufacturing sales and 33 percent of Insurance operating costs. The total was $143 million. It is $188 million now, but the company is three times the size and the percentage is one-fourth of what it was then.

If we had not gone after it, the PONC today would be, are you ready for this, $516 million. That is almost as much as sales were eight years ago. Here is the chart:

	Then	*Now*
Sales (000)	$540,000	$1,720,000
Manufacturing PONC	29.6%	9.2%
Insurance PONC	33%	6.4%
Company PONC (000)	143,000	188,240
Company profit after tax (000)	32,400	189,200

"So," said Foster, "the profit used to be about 20 percent of the PONC; now it is about equal. Is that a formula?"

Cynthia smiled.

"I think it must be, but you are the first person I ever heard express it. Makes sense."

"How about the specifics?" I asked. "Do you still do the breakdown of costs? How about rework and scrap?"

"Rework in Manufacturing and reprocessing in Insurance are still the primary costs. Scrap, interestingly enough, has disappeared. It is no longer socially acceptable. Eliminating it was almost exclusively a function of doing better process planning. And there is a parallel in computer programming: the better the specs are laid out, the less debugging time there is. I always thought debugging was much the same as scrap."

"So the pattern has actually been altered?" I asked.

"Very much so. Field service is really service, and not re-pair. Warranty costs are down, we haven't failed to pay our taxes on time, and the agent hot lines have become market-ing tools for customers to use in giving us business."

"Does this mean that people are really doing things right the first time?" said Foster. "Or are we finding problems ear-lier?"

"Mostly they have just become plain old prevention-oriented, Foster," said Cynthia. "It has taken all this time to get the concepts and the tools of prevention to become part of the infrastructure. But we see less and less scrambling around every day. We still make far too many mistakes, but people really care about them and take corrective action."

"What was the toughest part of making that happen?" I wondered.

"Getting middle managers to believe that we were serious about it all, and then teaching them how to implement. It was all rather flat for three years; then it suddenly zoomed. Phil is very patient about change. He says he learned it from you."

"How about the other characteristics?" said Foster. "We are pretty well up on growth. Most of that has been internal and has progressed very well. Can we talk about meeting customer needs?"

"That is one of the most interesting parts of this culture change. There has been a transformation both inside and outside. Our associates have begun to realize that they have customers inside the company, and that has helped us deal with the actual users of the products and services."

"Give me an example," said Foster.

"Field reporting comes to mind. We always had the problem that the field people would not tell everything they knew because they didn't want to be criticized, and because they thought the people back here wouldn't do anything anyway. Now the two groups have a completely different relationship and are working together to improve products and services," said Cynthia.

"I have many examples that we put together for *The Associates Magazine;* I will see that you get copies of those cases. It really is quite amazing."

"The lion and the lamb lie down together," said Foster. "Sometimes that is a good combination."

"Change management has been the most difficult one to grab hold of. The main problem is that not everyone recognizes change when he or she sees it, or understands that others need to know about it. Systems Integrity is in a constant state of battle trying to identify and then help control changes. It has been very frustrating," Cynthia replied.

"Has that been part of the education program they teach at Masters U? Is there anything to teach on it?" asked Foster.

"That has been another problem. We haven't had much difficulty obtaining the support we needed for all the other functions. Usually we just find the most effective source of information, a consulting firm, college, or individual, and then insert them and their material into the program."

She walked over and sat down.

"But it turns out that we are the experts in Systems Integrity, at least as far as we know. As I said before, it is very hard to have inside executives teach inside executives."

"I know two companies who have had a lot of experience with SI," I said. "That is where I stole the idea 10 years ago. I'll give you their names."

"Bless you," said Cynthia. "They must be keeping it a secret."

"Pride," she continued, "has turned out to be one of those things where everything you know about it turns out to be wrong, or at least not applicable.

"We went through every one of tried and true systems of communication, measurement, bonuses, talk groups, open doors and such. All of them helped, but it wasn't until we began to combine literal ownership with credible performance appraisal that things began to change," she noted.

"We know about the ownership part; the Board had to approve it. That has gone well?"

"Well is not the word for it. It has gone beautifully. Combining a stock purchase plan with the incentive compensation program and adding company funds to it like a thrift plan—well people can't believe how quickly it all builds up. Consequently they watch every penny from the inside and brag about the company on the outside.

"Turnover has dropped to virtually nothing, even in the sales areas."

"I don't remember it as well as you, George. Slow that down for me, Cynthia. Is this something we invented?" asked Foster.

"No, actually several companies had similar plans of stock ownership over the years. Sears, IBM, General Motors, Proctor and Gamble, I think, among others. Many still do things along this line. But most companies have dropped them because the employees were more interested in having the money now. Also the tax laws have not made them as attractive as before. We had to get a special ruling to make our plan possible.

"What we do is this: employees can put up to 6 percent of their gross pay into stock purchase; the company puts an additional 3 percent to go with that; they can put up to 50 percent of any incentive compensation they receive and are required to invest at least 25 percent of it. The company matches 20 percent of what they put in.

"All this is placed into company stock and grows tax-free over the years. Dividends are used to purchase more stock, and the whole package is insured so that if the value of the stock should go down, they would still get back what they put in plus interest."

"When can they pull it out?" asked Foster.

"There is a formula that requires so much capital in the plan and a vesting concerning the company funds. They are required to keep the equivalent of one year's pay and can draw a percentage of the vested out after that. It comes in handy when paying for college education," replied Cynthia. "So far," she finished, "there has been little withdrawal."

"And you credit this program with building the pride our associates have?" asked Foster.

"It has established a credibility we didn't have before, but it hasn't done the job all by itself. The new performance appraisal system, which Paul Christian helped us develop has been a big part of it. And then the supervisor training in human relations is a contributor. It is hard to believe how well-intentioned people can mistreat their associates when they just do not realize these things."

"I need to understand this performance appraisal system," I said. "It was just being proved out about the time I retired, and I really don't understand it. What it the best way to go about learning it?"

"Easiest thing in the world," said Cynthia. "I happen to have the forms right here. We can all evaluate each other."

She walked over to her briefcase and returned with three packages.

"We will pretend that I am your supervisor," she began. "These are the forms that go along with the exercise, and every job uses the same ones. We also have a film that explains the concept and system. I'll play that for you before we look at these papers. I think you'll find that the system is very easy to understand and work. The idea is to communicate, encourage, and aim. The associates call it CEA."

"Is it a very open subject?" asked Foster. "I mean if people have a nickname for the secret ingredients, then it must be well understood. That is unusual."

"The developers thought that there was too much mystery and professionalism in the normal performance appraisal systems. They also believed, and I agree, that the employee gets all the evaluation and advice. The company got only good news. This is different, as you will see.

"You will note, Foster, that I have learned to operate a VCR all by myself. My son taught me. Here we go."

The film came up in color with the title: *Career Building at Masters.* It opened in Phil's office. He was standing next to his white board, wearing shirtsleeves and smiling.

"I wanted to introduce this film," he said, "to make certain that every Masters associate understood how deeply committed management is to the concept and practice of career building.

"We set out a few years ago, with Chairman George Kales' encouragement, to see if we could foster the development of a corporate culture in which all associates would have concern for the company, loyalty to its traditions, and effectiveness in carrying out their work."

He turned to the board, and the three words (*concern, loyalty, effectiveness*) were displayed in a graphic. Then the word *concern* lifted off and became large, while the other two faded.

"*Concern,*" said Phil's voice, "is what we have for our families."

A happy family is romping around its front yard, then going back into the house. Everyone is very aware of one another; Dad opens the door for Mom; little sister gets a boost from big brother.

"All the members of the family want to be certain that the family as a whole is safe, nourished, and fulfilled. Everything they do has those concerns as a background. They all feel their responsibility, and they all have a voice in the organization."

The family is sitting around a table talking. Little sister has her say, and everyone listens.

Back to Phil's office.

"A business organization is a family also in that we depend on each other, and none of us can do the job by ourselves. We have to work together, listen to each other, and provide support."

Loyalty came out of the graphic, and the voiceover continued.

"Loyalty comes from an appreciation of tradition and relationships. It is similar to how many of us feel toward the schools or other organizations we were in during our developmental years [shot of ivy-covered campus with students walking about].

"I still feel a special loyalty to the Navy where I spent several years.

"We develop a loyalty because the organization helped us develop ourselves and stood by us when we were unsure of ourselves, or needed some base to relate to. I went back to a high school reunion recently and really appreciated the familiarity I felt with the grounds and building. Some of the teachers even remembered me. A great deal of it was just as I remembered."

Efficiency lifted to the center of the screen [scenes of people working with computer terminals, manufacturing lines operating, salespeople greeting customers, and the outsides of three different office buildings and two manufacturing plants].

"A company, like a family or a college, has to produce in order to be successful. It has to grow [children being measured against the wall in the kitchen, new football stadium under construction, little sister in kindergarten cap and gown]; it has to manage its resources [Dad paying bills, son mowing yard, Mom patching some torn clothes, college library checking over books, Navy painting a ship].

"We have to keep progressing in our capabilities both personal and corporate.

"Every individual involved in the organization needs to be able to look forward to becoming all he or she is able to become. The company should be in a position to help the individual create a career. A great deal of this help can come from providing educational support [adults in classroom], from providing on-the-job training [two people at a terminal, one teaching], and from providing counseling for those in specific situations."

The graphic spelled out: *Career Building*.

Phil was walking through an office where people were sitting at desks working. As he talked, that shot dissolved and he was walking through a factory.

"All of us are individuals, and as such we are different. We have separate ambitions and capabilities. We want to do different things; we are not all the same. Not by a long shot. We have our own ideas about what careers are best for ourselves" [scenes: football players crashing, cheerleaders cheering, executive walking with briefcase, chef, secretary, medical personnel, salesperson, machine operator, truck driver, draftsperson]. The voiceover continued during all this.

"Nothing works well unless everyone who participates gets something from it [little sister in kitchen, with cake makings all over her after helping mother, licking the icing bowl]. In the case of the Career Building program, the individual has the opportunity to grow according to personal abilities, and the company has the maximum use of the talents and energies of its associates.

"The basis of Career Building is a personal evaluation built on three blocks."

Individual (male) goes into conference room where the supervisor is waiting. Both carry a folder. They shake hands and chat familiarly as they open their individual folders and exchange one sheet each.

"The blocks are: communication, encouragement, aim. Communication relates to the job that is being accomplished at the present time. In this demonstration the associate has completed the form by describing his present job as he understands it and has rated himself on how well it is being done.

"The supervisor has performed an identical evaluation and the two exchange sheets. As you will see when you look at the form, it is not complex and has as its sole purpose serving as a base for two people to talk about a subject.

"It is here that they learn whether they share a common understanding of what the work is, and it is here where they find out if they view the results the same way."

[All the while the two people are comparing notes. Now the film picks up their discussion.]

ASSOCIATE: I haven't been clear on that point, Frank. In dealing with suppliers I have been careful to make certain that they understood the requirements as I got them from Engineering or Manufacturing. But I haven't done much about seeing if these are really what engineering or manufacturing really want.

SUPERVISOR: I know it seems that they should be clear before sending the order over to you in Purchasing. But, as you can see, the rejection level of the material you order is higher than normal. The major cause of nonconformance is wrong requirements.

ASSOCIATE: But we are able to get it cleared up in most cases and wind up using the material just like it is.

SUPERVISOR: True, but in the meantime we have you, an engineer, the quality people, the supplier, and sometimes myself wrapped up in it. It seems like a lot of hassle that could be prevented.

ASSOCIATE: I sure would like that. So you are suggesting that I spend more time getting the requirements clear up front before placing the order? That makes sense, I wonder why I never got into that before?

SUPERVISOR: Last year when you moved over to Purchasing, we were suddenly taking over the buying for the Lansdown and Integarden plants. You didn't get the "big brother" treatment that we usually lay out for new purchasing agents.

ASSOCIATE: So how do I get this straight now?

SUPERVISOR: If you agree, I will arrange for you to sit in on a couple of "up-front" discussions this week. Then we can talk again about it to see if there are further questions. The format is laid out, but it does take some experience. I like to bring the supplier into the session, too, at least into the second one.

ASSOCIATE: This has been a big help Frank.

SUPERVISOR: We'll continue to do this on a regular basis, Marvin, we have to make certain we both understand your job and your progress the same way. The feedback I get from your customers in Engineering and Manufacturing is that they believe you take the responsibility seriously and are concerned that they receive what they need. I haven't asked any of the suppliers yet, but if it is all right with you, I will get input from them before our next session. You are doing very well. Now we need to talk about encouragement. [They trade forms.]

SUPERVISOR: As you know, this form, and the discussion that goes with it, are designed to let us talk about any help you might think you need in order to both do your present job better and at the same time develop skills or knowledge for future assignments; also it lets me suggest things that would provide improvement. You first—are you having any problems with company-controlled items, such as management direction?

ASSOCIATE: No, everyone is available when I need help or information, and I haven't been whipped lately. One thing I need to get more information on is the stock purchase plan. I used to understand it, but now there are a few added wrinkles. All for the best I hear, but I need to get clear on it.

SUPERVISOR: Human Resources is having regular classes, and there is a new brochure that just came out. You might want to send it to your financial advisor too.

ASSOCIATE: Good. Next is personal performance. I hate to admit it, but I find I am having trouble writing letters. I never had to do much of that before. I watch Harold Rawlings, and he just bats them out. Mine don't even make sense the first time around, and when I do get them done, they sound stilted and formal.

SUPERVISOR: That's a problem many of us have. So many, in fact, that there is a special course in it at the Educational Institute. I like the way they do it. They start off with the basics and lead you through. I went to a different course on that once, and they had us bring our old letters and tore us up. It was like having someone try to fix a bad golf swing. You can talk to the institute directly, or I will get hold of them for you.

ASSOCIATE: I can do it. I hadn't known about that course.

SUPERVISOR: Perhaps you don't know about all the things that are available. Have you seen this catalog before?

ASSOCIATE: I recognize it, but I never studied it. After I went to orientation and then to quality class at the institute, I figured that was all they had for me. Then later, of course, I took Purchasing.

SUPERVISOR: Next year Purchasing II will be available. It will include things we don't have now, like zero inventory control and the up-front sessions we were talking about. Any other problems?

ASSOCIATE: I just want to make sure that I am making a solid contribution to the company. I realize that I will never be president; I just don't have the education or the smarts for that. I do appreciate your being open and direct with me.

SUPERVISOR: Don't sell yourself short. It is good to recognize our own limits, but sometimes we are not the best people to do that. It is true that we only have one president and that limits the availability of the job. But there are a lot of other career paths in the company. Why don't we go on to *aim?*

ASSOCIATE: About two years ago my unattainable aim was to someday be a purchasing agent, and here I am. I think it is possible to handle more responsibility after I really understand this job. That is going to take a few years.

SUPERVISOR: First things first, of course. However, we have identified a couple of objectives so far today.

ASSOCIATE: Right, reducing—actually eliminating—rejections that I caused and learning to write effective business letters. I have a lot to learn about purchasing, but I think we could cut that present rate, which is 6 percent, in half by the end of the year and then eliminate it altogether six months after that. It is a matter of supplier selection, clear requirements, and coordination. All those are manageable, but I'm going to need some help.

SUPERVISOR: Why don't you give me a plan, and I'll see what I can do to run interference for you, if you should need it.

As the two men continued their conversation, the sound of their voices ended and Phil came back on the screen.

"That was a much shortened session. Its purpose was to give you the idea of the Career Building process. Planned sessions are held for each individual twice a year, but the relationship between supervisors and associates is continual. The Executive Committee of the Board of Directors does the same exercise with me.

"You will receive more detailed instruction concerning how to handle the paperwork that goes along with the process. Thank you."

As the credits began to roll by, Cynthia stopped the video and rewound it.

"That sounds like it actually might work," said Foster. "All the ones I have been associated with made people mad or defensive or both. The Education Institute plays a big part in carrying through on aims. Do they teach everything themselves?"

"Oh no," replied Cynthia. "At least half of the courses are conducted out in the world at other schools. We coordinate the subjects, do some checking on their worth, and poll the students on results.

"Most of the ones taught inside the institute are conducted by consulting firms or specialists. That leaves probably 15 percent that are originated and conducted by Masters personnel. The functional subjects, like Purchasing, Marketing, and such are laid out and taught by those who do the function for a living. But we also bring in specialists," she explained.

"That institute must cost a fortune," I suggested.

"There are only six permanent employees, worldwide. But it all does cost money, about $50 per associate per year, or a million and a half dollars. The only way to make it cost more is to try to do it all ourselves," she replied.

"Building a training empire gives you the worst of two worlds," said Foster. "The pros want to teach everything, and they can't know everything. And they always wind up with a massive facility that binds you to it."

After the session Foster and I went to a nearby restaurant for some lunch. Cynthia had other plans, which let us have the opportunity to finish our conversation.

"I've been poking around for some time now, George," said Foster, "and I have come to the conclusion that all this is actually coming true. The report card she showed us is accurate, and the systems seem to be working. People are becoming prevention-minded and working that way."

"I agree, Foster," I said. "And I have to say that I wanted it to turn out like this, but I wasn't certain the management team was ready to take it all seriously.

"As you know, it is possible to do just about everything as long as everyone wants to. This business is not something that can be improved by anything except example and education. I wasn't sure they were ready.

"They had taken on expansion, and were doing it right; and they were getting new products that the customers loved; they were even becoming interested in controlling expenses. Now that is something everyone is for, in other areas."

"But they didn't relate to being Eternally Successful?" asked Foster.

"Well it sounds like 'more of the same,' that's all. One more noble cause that we all have to strive for. But now I see them all just doing the things that make sense, the actions everyone would like to do but never has time."

"It all comes down to something we have said all along," I philosophized.

"Which is?" asked Foster.

"Take care of the employees and the customers; the rest will take care of itself."

"The check's on me, Plato," said Foster.

And he picked it up.

PART 3
The Quest Continues

17

Systems Integrity

The best way to understand something is to become involved in its development and implementation. That is probably why most of us learn selectively. We do well with the things we can touch, even if only figuratively. Once we have worked something through, we can know enough about it to argue. Before that, only opinions are brought into the discussion.

Quality has to be caused, not controlled. As I noted earlier, the basic concepts of dealing with quality have caused a lot of trouble over the years. It became necessary to learn to be resourceful in order to cope with products and services that did not even pretend to be what was ordered. When organizations came along that actually did what they said they were going to do, the market was theirs.

To learn from this, we must deliberately incorporate safeguards of prevention into new strategies. To provide an experience of doing this, I thought I would take us through the establishment of a new strategy in a company and show how the concept of Systems Integrity can help bring it off.

The company I was thinking about is a management consulting firm whose main activity revolves around educating the management and employees of client companies, as well as supporting their efforts at improvement. The company deals with many clients all over the free world and is considered the best in its field. Its primary asset, actually, is its credibility.

As the business grew, the management took the company public in order to provide funds for expanding the company to Europe and the Far East. The major cost items were: training new consultant-instructors, translating current material into seven languages, setting up new classrooms and offices, and developing new material.

As the offices came online, the demand from clients matched company growth, and the organization found itself continually struggling to keep up. The key blocking consideration was in the training of new professionals. It took several months to bring them to a level where they could be exposed to clients in the classroom. Expenses were rising because of the amount of internal support required and the cost of using people from the United States to work in Europe on a temporary basis.

At the same time pressures were being put forth for the company to establish offices and educational activities in India, Korea, Taiwan, and Latin America. Other locations would not be far behind all this because a constant stream of inquiries came into the company's offices. It was a genuine good-news–bad-news situation.

The good news was that many companies were interested in obtaining the services offered; the bad news was that all this was very expensive and time-consuming to start up and establish. Management time was deeply involved in growth, which left running current operations at a lower level. As a result some of the basic domestic activities were beginning to be neglected.

The financial community rewarded all this by dropping the price of the company's stock and refusing to recognize the long-term potential of the organization. The senior executives went out and explained it all, but no one seemed to understand. The investment groups drifted off to something they could explain to their customers, and the individual buyers looked for something going in the other direction.

The Board asked for a new approach, and the management team took itself away for a few days to think about a way of growing that would be more profitable, involve less hassle, and still provide the clients with the services they needed. The group also was mindful that it was necessary to provide sufficient incentive and reward for the key professionals and managers inside the company.

After much discussion and reflection, the group came to the conclusion that the company should consider a radical approach: it should sell the rights to "deliver" the products and find current personnel and perhaps other consulting companies who would be willing to do those jobs while operating under a strict set of rules.

The company's educational products lend themselves to this approach since they have been laid out in two basic areas: those which are taught to management face-to-face; and those taught to the employees through films and workbooks. In the first case, the professionals teach the course assisted by films; in the second, client employees are trained to conduct the course, using films and workbooks. All material is sold or leased to the client, and of course this is where the money is produced.

Face-to-face education covers about 3 percent of the people, and the rest is facilitated by client instructors who have been through special classes.

The management team used as an example the soft drink companies who sell syrup to their bottlers and use stringent controls to see that everything is used correctly. The bottlers become wealthy, the clients are well served, and the mother company prospers. It seemed a perfect pattern.

A holding company would be formed, and subsidiaries could be set up to permit local ownership. Some of the company's employees could purchase the rights in their areas, and in a few cases other consulting firms could be permitted to participate. One company had offices and people all over the world and was well suited to take on this venture while doing it properly. Then the company itself could concentrate on developing new material, promoting the products themselves, and making certain that there was no adulteration of the products. Everything had to be the same every place, exactly the same.

This last point was the one that concerned the Board most—which is what brought up the discussion of Systems Integrity and how it has been designed to prevent problems in that area. Everyone agreed that the integrity of the product was imperative. And that integrity had to apply to the delivery as well as the content. The clients had to be absolutely certain that they were getting our best, every time. They had to trust those who were doing the delivery.

The chief financial officer and the chairperson were assigned to work out a system for establishing the "delivery rights" organizations. One part of this was to determine the initial fee each operation would be required to pay in order to obtain the franchise. This fee would not apply to any future expenses and would not be refundable. It was going to cost some money to set up the system that would train the new professionals and supply the franchise operations with material. But also they wanted to be sure that the company was going to be compensated for the risk it was taking with its credibility.

The other part concerned fee sharing for products delivered to clients. Should the franchise operators pay a portion of what they receive, or should they pay for their inventory? It was essential that prices be consistent to all clients in all countries.

Systems Integrity was going to concentrate on three areas:

1. It would continually review the material development and supply system to assure that changes were incorporated in an orderly and controlled fashion and that the copyrights were properly respected.

2. It would evaluate the training of instructor-consultants, including using classroom evaluations by students. It would make certain that noncompete and noninterference contracts were held and complied with by all.

3. It would continually review the confidence of clients in the education and counseling they were receiving and conduct continuing evaluations to be sure that the results received were excellent.

When all these characteristics are laid out on a spreadsheet and subjected to measurement and analysis, management will have a clear picture of the status and know where to take corrective action.

In addition to these operational considerations it is essential that prospective franchises pass financial evaluations and are subject to regular auditing of financial results. This overall strategy should permit the company to increase its profits by a factor of 10 while reducing its staff. The company would continue to teach the executives of client companies and the professionals of the franchise operations.

The Systems Integrity Department is not large, representing about 2 percent of the staff. It is independent, reporting to the Audit Committee of the Board through the chairperson's office. This assures that no influence can be applied to its decisions.

The key to a successful Systems Integrity operation is selecting leaders who really understand the products of the company and the intent of its culture, then taking experienced operational people and training them in the internal auditing concepts and techniques.

Such operations should stay away from traditional quality techniques except for areas such as publishing where they may be applicable. Many franchises may desire to do their own printing and so will need in-process evaluation.

What SI brings to a company is an executive-level measurement and analysis that has never existed before. Financial reports have always been around in depth, if behind the times. SI can be real-time. There is no reason that reporting cannot be fed into a software system that permits readouts on anyone's desk. Then no one gets into very much trouble before it is known.

The type of system management described here produces consistent product delivery, controlled change, and yes, a sense of integrity about the entire organization.

If there is anything noticeable about an eternally successful organization, it is its integrity.

Guidelines
for Browsers

Unfortunately no one is against preventing; it's just that they don't have time right now.   *vii*

Outside of hanging around with a sign that said: "Repent, the end is near," my planned approach has been as always low key and fairly subtle.   *vii*

Through these years I have come to realize that there is a lot involved in running a company that has little to do with the content of the management systems.   *viii*

If we take care of the customers and the employees, everything else takes care of itself.   *viii*

It is hard to find an organization that both customers and employees regard with continuous affection and appreciation.   *viii*

Executives cannot be sold into being serious about quality; they have to make the decision themselves, and in their own time.   *viii*

There is no substitute for combat when it comes to learning the difference between keeping your head down and raising it.   *ix*

Not everything is as it seems.   *3*

The primary measurement characteristic was how much

money the company made; the second was how long it had been around. *4*

I had always assumed that everyone else knew a lot more about everything than I did. *4*

We are all customers and entitled to not be disappointed. *5*

The criterion for being a successful person was the ability to get something done. *5*

If one could produce, and was a halfway reasonable person, there was an open road ahead. *5*

Hardly anyone knew anything about what was happening except in his or her own area of work. *6*

It doesn't take long in any organization before one can have a broader view of what is happening than most other folks. *6*

It was all right not to know—at least the first time—and one could dig into a subject until it was clear. *6*

Negative numbers had brackets around them. *6*

The slightest sign of uncertainty or "weaselwording" was enough to bring forth intense questioning. *7*

Knowing how to handle an international managerial problem was of little help when it came to figuring out leases in Central Florida. *8*

Quality is a serious matter and should be treated that way. *9*

My mind is tuned to gathering bits and pieces of information that eventually glump together into some sort of awareness. *9*

We all comprehend only a small portion of the complete picture. *9*

Each company's GMM may be equivalent to only a gossip session. *9*

So how come that successful organization does not maintain that level of accomplishment continuously? *9*

We see many cases where the apparently invincible organization becomes vulnerable seemingly overnight. *10*

The entire Japanese automobile industry, for instance, could have been purchased, or joined as a partner, for peanuts in the early 1970s.   *10*

Being convinced that one knows the whole picture is the surest way to failure, as we all know.   *10*

Someone or some group or some system has to actually run things.   *10*

The planning system that worked so well doesn't work any more; customers who were unswervingly loyal are committing economic adultery; the apolitical environment in the company has collapsed, and nest building is going on everywhere.   *10*

The butterfly has become a sloth.   *11*

Most organizations have what appear to me to be suicidal tendencies.   *11*

Debt begins to rise; accounts receivable age faster; bright young people begin to drift off to other companies; a huge new headquarters building gets built; customers are becoming neglected; housekeeping noticeably deteriorates; and management doesn't seem to notice.   *11*

It takes a lot of cooperative foolishness to reach this point.   *11*

Most problems are avoidable but are rarely seen by those involved.   *11*

Organizations don't start out to be losers.   *11*

The organization is turning brown around the edges, and there seems to be little reason for it.   *12*

People can't last forever; the body eventually wears out. There is no way to prevent that from happening. But organizations have no need to die.   *12*

Growing and maturing provide their own pain, but it should be a pleasant sensation, worth the effort.   *13*

Companies and people tend to fail eventually when they become locked into one format or culture.   *13*

When the employees and suppliers of an organization do things correctly on a routine basis; when customers are pleased that their needs are anticipated and met; when growth is internally generated, profitable, and planned; when change is welcomed and implemented to advantage; and when everyone enjoys working there—the foundation of an eternally successful organization exists. *13*

Society does not admire failure. *13*

The personal agenda that individuals select lies within themselves but can be influenced dramatically by the goals of the organization and the obligations of the individuals to it. *13*

The most consistently successful of all enterprises seem to be those that are "family" managed. *13*

Professional executives are more likely to be loyal to the company and its products than to the stockholders. *14*

I cannot recall a single meeting conversation about doing anything for the stockholders in all my years of working for large companies. *14*

Executives know they can move on to another company and will not even be missed after a few months. *14*

Colleges and some other nonprofit organizations muddle through over the years. *14*

Companies can completely reverse themselves in a week. What was important becomes repulsive. *15*

Family businesses sometimes come apart because of disagreements between family members that have nothing to do with business. *15*

Colleges fail to grow or respond because the administrators are intimidated by the faculty or vice versa. *15*

Conventional organizations fail for all the conventional reasons we read about in *Fortune, Forbes,* and *Business Week*—mostly executive ego. *15*

The organization can survive only when its immune system is designed to operate automatically. *15*

People do things right routinely.   *18*

Growth is profitable and steady.   *18*

Customer needs are anticipated.   *18*

Change is planned and managed.   *18*

People are proud to work there.   *18*

As the company gets easier to manage, pitfalls are avoided because there are no secrets, and the personal success of the manager is assured.   *16*

Every organization has some success at some time, even if only a great opening night.   *17*

In business, past is not necessarily prologue.   *17*

Nothing can be taken as permanent.   *17*

Organizations don't begin with a clean sheet of paper each year.   *18*

People and systems get entrenched, so much that they exist only for themselves.   *18*

The eternally successful organization does not have to contend with uneven times and is assured that survival is only an academic question.   *18*

In the ESO, wall reading is a requirement.   *19*

Every business changes every day in some way.   *19*

There is no oil fairy.   *19*

"It costs so much to ship steel from Japan to the United States that we never have to worry about it."   *19*

Half the market went to others in the process.   *20*

This industry fought for tariff protection instead of learning how to make (TV) sets that were reliable.   *20*

The gains made by research were wasted by "commodity" thinking.   *20*

Variable product integrity turned this into a risky business.   *20*

Airlines are run by people who have never flown like normal folks.   *20*

Practicing medicine is no fun anymore.   *20*

We will become a nation of renters and landlords.   *21*

People are too busy wondering to do much worshiping.   *25*

No one is doing well since none of them remember how to do service properly.   *21*

Every town seems to have too much commercial property.   *22*

Very little thought has been given to the possibility that people could ever be counted on to do things right routinely.   *25*

Basic training in every trade counts on browbeating to get the novice's attention.   *25*

Many of the worst situations are caused by those whose devotion overrode the laws of the land or the prudence of their position.   *25*

We have all seen situations in which a group of people were brought together in an environment where it was important that things be done correctly, and it actually came about.   *26*

The outstanding teams are invariably said to have accomplished their victories by "execution."   *26*

Each person performed his assigned task completely, at the correct time.   *26*

Very few of the great leaders ever get through their career without failing, sometimes dramatically.   *27*

Most people have good intentions but don't produce the results they dream about.   *27*

Talent does not work in isolation for most of us.   *28*

We can spend our whole lives underachieving.   *28*

The great discoveries are usually obvious.   *29*

Higher ups have "mission statements" which sound good but are hard to measure.   *29*

It doesn't take very long before a great deal of the organization's work has very little to do with the main objectives of the business.   *29*

Selecting the right person for the right job is the largest part of coaching.   *30*

The hidden component is "heart."   *30*

Players, in all sports, spend their entire careers on the fundamentals.   *30*

The measurement of job performance in most jobs is subjective, revolving around energy, attitude, and output.   *30*

The difference between a mediocre career and an outstanding experience is the concept of doing the job completely.   *31*

Just being honest is not enough.   *32*

The essential ingredient is executive integrity.   *33*

The reason quality is a problem rather than an asset lies in the management policy and style of the company, not in the tools of measurement and control.   *33*

The trivial many are considered not worthy of attention and are soon forgotten.   *34*

The quality professionals have been holding their fingers in the dikes all these years.   *34*

Quality means conformance to requirements   *35*

Quality comes from prevention.   *35*

Quality performance standard is Zero Defects.   *35*

Quality measurement is the Price of Nonconformance.   *35*

Companies reflect the standards of their leaders.   *35*

It takes several years to go from conviction through conversion.   *36*

In 1066 William the Conqueror and his Normans invaded Britain.   *37*

There were no investment bankers involved, so William

really had no idea what the Anglo-Saxon balance sheet looked like. *38*

It takes a long while for the anger created by a hostile take-over to disperse at the senior levels. *38*

For the survivors, their "life of quiet desperation" goes on much as before. The new leadership treats them no better or worse than the previous. *38*

Companies (and nonprofits, too) have to grow if for no other reason than to accommodate the increased expenses that develop over the years. *38*

There is nothing more discouraging to shareholders or the public than a "flat" performance. *39*

Getting all the people to work together whether they want to or not is where the deal becomes sticky. *39*

Marriage between two people is at best a 50:50 shot. *40*

In any merger a dangerous wedding night is created by the premise that the new management will run the operation more efficiently than the old one. *40*

The airline customer has to be obedient. *40*

The hotel customer has a great deal of choice. *40*

The rent-a-car customer is seen for a few hurried but brief moments at each end of the relationship. *41*

Travel service organizations deal with clients on a personal basis, even with package tours. *41*

Credit card organizations are all paperwork; no one ever sees a customer face-to-face. *41*

Nobody loves those they owe. *41*

Years of running a restaurant do little to prepare one for managing an airport car rental location. *42*

Strategy is one of the most overworked words in the management vocabulary. *42*

Management has to lead and in some cases drag people along. *43*

Strategies have to begin with an understanding of what the business consists of, what the ingredients are, what the opportunities are, and where the problems lie. *43*

These new computer systems are very costly, but I don't know how we can get along without them. *44*

Our traditional market is shrinking with no effort being made to broaden it, and the cost of sales is rising. *44*

The Board is interested in raising our growth to 15 percent a year with profits to match, and Board members recognize that achieving such a goal may take a while. *45*

Everytime I hear the word *mission* I think of a big, complicated, political-sounding document that everyone nods about but no one takes seriously. *45*

The mission has to be bigger than one task? *46*

I think we need to take a look at what our customers are telling us. *46*

The only way to grow properly is to provide something that someone is going to buy. *46*

Our mission is to provide the homeowner with the full protection of insurance, offer competitive rates, and do it all so efficiently that we can make money off the investment portfolio. *56*

Apparently we are off the track as a company. *47*

Grow where the business is; don't try to make a market where none exists. *47*

Debt is not your friend. *48*

Certainly the customer comes first. Who doesn't know that? *49*

There are many other customers along the way who bleed off the intensity of devotion to the final user. *49*

Analysts live by the quarter and would prefer to do it by the hour. *49*

Those who run the companies find themselves with many

"customers" who affect the state of the organization in different ways.   *50*

Success comes from customers, not evaluators.   *50*

If we can clearly aim our effort at genuine customer identification and satisfaction and combine that with actually knowing what their needs are, we will stand a good chance of being eternally successful.   *50*

If one picks the wrong customers, examines them carefully to determine their needs, and then delivers the exact requirements—it will all come to naught.   *51*

Not too many mothers buy Wheaties cereal for themselves.   *51*

I suspect the Sears Roebuck catalog opened more eyes than anything before or since.   *52*

There are so many choices today that customers can change their way of doing things overnight.   *52*

We all know that nobody's customers stay put.   *52*

There is no way to anticipate what people are going to do when it concerns their buying and social habits.   *53*

I know of no one in the book business who can tell what people will buy.   *53*

Mature companies perform market surveys and agonize over the results, trying to determine what is going on out there. Then they take thoughtful action and miss the target most of the time.   *53*

The employees who deal with real customers develop a sense of what those customers need or want.   *55*

But how to find out from the employees?   *55*

Customers change for many reasons besides the product or its price.   *55*

It is hard to tell one bank from another when it comes to products.   *55*

This may be the last big order we get from Hartley if we

don't learn how to deliver "Just-in-Time" inventory style.   *57*

Anyone who has been in the business world knows that salespeople sometimes come back with a tale about how what is going on is not their fault.   *57*

Business executives have to be like the young swain who is attentive to every mood and interest swing his beloved expresses, no matter how discreetly or modestly they are displayed.   *57*

Managers have to interrogate both clients and employees continually.   *58*

And that is what it is all about: relationships.   *58*

Concepts of marketing or selling can become obsolete quickly if the customer is forgotten for a few minutes.   *59*

The senior managers of any organization have to continually be forced to keep up.   *59*

Relationships determine success.   *59*

Today's correct concepts are good only for today.   *59*

Top management should know some customers personally.   *59*

Don't let the internal customers take precedence over those with the real money.   *59*

Advertising should build confidence in the company first and the product second.   *59*

Our customers want us to do something different; I think we need to at least find out for sure.   *61*

We have to continually look at the concepts we use as our operating philosophy.   *62*

No matter how it turns out, I am looking forward to my brush with reality.   *62*

Nothing seems to be permanent. Everything has to be reviewed continually.   *64*

All that is taken care of before it ever gets here. Each supplier has agreed to deliver defect-free material, and we have worked with them, as necessary, to make certain that happens. And they have to do it by prevention, not by adding a bunch of appraisal functions.   *66*

Keeping up-to-date without wearing yourself out or spending into oblivion is very difficult.   *69*

More harm comes from automatically rejecting anything new than from giving it a fair evaluation.   *70*

What brought all this about was the realization that a company, being a living, growing entity, was in a continuous state of change just like a person.   *71*

We decided to look at change as being our friend instead of a pain in the neck.   *71*

Keeping out of trouble instead of learning how to solve every new disaster is the idea.   *71*

Change is our friend when we manage it; it is a disaster if we just change to change.   *71*

The functions of business organizations encompass many different disciplines.   *72*

One person's adventure is another person's frustration.   *73*

Change has never been thought of as something that required formalization, or for that matter could even be handled in a planned fashion.   *73*

Change is a serious business; it is incredibly expensive to do things wrong and over all the time.   *74*

Companies having quality control functions will find that it takes fewer people to run Systems Integrity, with much more effect.   *74*

The world keeps on going around whether we want it to or not.   *75*

Not every change is good for us; not every change is bad.   *75*

Managing change means that everyone has to be involved enough to know what he or she will have to do about it.   *75*

Systems Integrity deals with each part of the organization and its relationships with others.   *75*

Watch out for changes recommended eagerly by those who would profit from it.   *75*

We all have watched as organizations were transformed from a place everyone loved into one nobody could stand—all in only a few months.   *77*

Changing love to hate doesn't take very long. Returning from hate to love can require years.   *77*

The reasons managers work to turn their people against them are not always easily understood.   *77*

But why should business leaders want their employees to hate the place, or at best be uncomfortable there?   *77*

Why do they permit managers to harass the employees?   *77*

Unfortunately there are only so many slots whose natural position is above the fray.   *78*

Guests have to do what you want to do; customers can call the tune.   *78*

There is little to be proud of personally when everything is supplied.   *79*

Executives recognize the importance of pride, of course, and most want their employees to have it.   *79*

People have to deal with the professionals instead of the principles, and the crassness of procedural control and impersonal assignment enters the world.   *80*

Naturally the office staff began to think that something desperate was going on when the chiefs began shutting the door.   *80*

The really good people start preparing to disappear when leadership begins to have credibility problems.   *81*

Each loss of pride produces an exodus that leaves the organization in the hands of the less competent—which is nothing to be proud of.   *81*

Changing the unproud to the proud is a complex and unyielding operation.   *81*

It is much better to start out proud and keep working to improve the feeling, stopping short of arrogance, of course.   *81*

Our biggest problems are getting good people and figuring out what the customers want.   *82*

There is a great parallel between preventing heart disease and running a successful company.   *83*

The whole approach of "wellness" for the person is wrapped around prevention.   *84*

Customers are not as forgiving as our bodies are.   *84*

Just as we have to deal with the whole body, so we have to deal with the whole company.   *84*

Success is rather predictable. What you put in is what you get out.   *85*

I would never send something to a customer that was not what we had promised to send.   *86*

As long as things can go out without being right, no one will believe you are serious about it.   *86*

That is the same problem people have with preventing heart disease. They see no relationship between life habits and health.   *86*

People do not take pride in a sloppy work area. And that habit extends over to dealing with customers.   *87*

Managers set the code by the way they behave and by the condition of their offices and attire.   *87*

As long as they were sitting around complaining about things instead of working hard with those employees and customers, the company slowly drifted into sloppy habits.   *88*

The tacky environment produced tacky thinking and everything really did get worse.   *88*

Pride brings out the best in people; arrogance brings out the worst.   *88*

The tradition behind the memento is the important factor.   *88*

Over the years many labor organizations became so concerned with political power, with intimidating management, and with continual increases in wages and benefits that they lost touch with reality.   *89*

But many labor leaders lost sight of the purpose of the unions.   *89*

There are more jobs available, which isn't much consolation if you are a diehard steel mill worker.   *90*

But now management is beginning to re-create, in the knowledge areas, what previous generations of leaders established in the broader field of labor.   *90*

People will just not give their all to an organization that won't give them proper consideration.   *90*

The organization has to have clear goals and objectives that the employees can respect.   *90*

The management has to be consistently dedicated to having everyone understand and be able to meet the performance requirements that will cause the organization to reach those goals and objectives.   *90*

Any downturn or unfortunate incident must be faced openly and directly.   *91*

In short: "Do unto others as you would have others do unto you."   *91*

Today the half-life of a CEO is about one year.   *95*

Eternal vigilance is now the price of success.   *95*

It is necessary to prepare for the future continually.   *95*

Staying out of the quicksand is much better than getting a good deal on a towing contract.   *95*

Almost everyone has some failing or problem that could be improved if he or she only recognizes that it exists.   *96*

It doesn't take long before the people running a place become convinced that it is their own personality and personal charm that causes everything to hum in unison.   *97*

The marketing plans are not the least bit people-sensitive; even Human Resources doesn't seem interested in the troops.   *97*

We have been talking about the actions necessary to give this corporation the opportunity to be eternally successful.   *97*

People who see to your every need when you visit their home act like tax collectors in their office.   *97*

Corporate wellness was really what we were trying to cause.   *98*

"Concern" applies primarily to the people, the "loyalty" to the institution itself, and the "efficiency" to management skills. All of those can be identified, measured, and caused.   *98*

We can't get executives to really become involved in something unless they feel ownership.   *99*

We have to have a long-range concept for managing that is ground inside the minds of our leaders.   *99*

We can make certain they understand how seriously we need to learn how to practice management in order to secure the future for this organization.   *100*

We have eliminated all separate dining in every facility throughout the corporation.   *102*

Instead of a place of convenience and communication, it had become a source of controversy and disruption.   *102*

I think we are going to have to recognize that the executive dining room is no longer good for the company.   *102*

I decided that management was going to have to work harder to make itself clear, on everything.   *103*

The finance business isn't what it used to be.   *104*

You wheeler-dealers always think about positioning products, but you forget people.   *104*

Malls are for advertising, explaining, and getting them interested.   *104*

Whenever I hear some retailers talking about how they never made any money, I know it is time to lock up my assets.   *105*

Retailing is the real world.   *105*

Ours is a nickel here, dime there business.   *105*

Some people look at a store and see counters full of merchandise. I look at those same counters and see trays full of dollar bills, my dollar bills. The idea is to exchange mine for the customer's.   *106*

I have to grind my raw material, melt it, pour it, roll it, cool it, package it, deliver it, and then listen to the complaints. And we are lucky if we make 2 percent after tax.   *106*

Most of the deficiencies that are found require complicated and deep changes in the way the business is run.   *107*

Can you imagine handling 400-million-share days with ballpoint pens?   *107*

Our growth has been good, but the customer is a dim second in our thoughts and no one has hugged me lately to say what a wonderful place this is to work.   *108*

The "not doing things right" is probably the clearest datum we have.   *109*

Our program was aimed at the bottom of the organization, and management never did get involved. We also learned that you can't teach executives from inside a company.   *109*

We made 12 percent pretax last year in Masters and spent three or four times that doing things wrong.   *110*

Although we do a lot of customer contact and surveying, almost none of that gets to any of the operating areas.   *110*

We received a unanimous agreement that the company does a terrible job in both causing and controlling change.   *111*

Management acceptance of SI has not been that terrific. Managers feel threatened.   *111*

It doesn't take much to threaten management.   *111*

The biggest concerns here related to employees not feeling as if they are a part of the organization and wondering about the future of the company.   *112*

Once a company gets past a hundred people, communication has to be forced.   *112*

Taking things into myself has always been a problem for me.   *113*

Frankly, I had never heard of the Price of Nonconformance before a few months ago, but it is really a powerful tool.   *113*

So we spend $91 million doing things wrong and $1.3 million preventing spending the $91 million? That seems backward.   *114*

White collar workers are about 50 percent effective.   *115*

A lot of these costs have to come from lack of change control, people not having pride in the organization, customer data not being utilized, and such.   *115*

This has been the best meeting I have ever attended.   *116*

We needed to take positive action and didn't have time to fool around.   *118*

There are consultants and consultants. I don't want a bunch of people who disrupt operations and stick around forever.   *118*

My experience has been that companies make the contact points with consultants too low in the organization.   *118*

Consultants you can get rid of and no one cares, but cutting out staff is a big deal.   *119*

The reason this outfit is not going strong today is that it thought it was infallible.   *119*

They thought all they had to do was keep track, pound down

the problems, and acquire companies to fill in any cracks that might appear in a product line. *119*

No managers would encourage people to do things wrong the first time, but they don't do much about helping them get it done right the first time. *120*

Everyone makes changes, but very few take care to inject them into the bloodstream of the company. *120*

We all want people to be proud of their work, but we don't do much about making it happen. *120*

It would be prohibitive to have processes without rework; you'd have to throw away what produces a large part of our margin. *122*

The system we have has been working well for a long time. We don't like to change what doesn't need changing. *123*

You believe that the quality issue is exaggerated; you think that the customer is listened to; you believe that we handle change okay—it's just that the people don't listen; and you think that people are really proud to work here, and the analysis was wrong. *124*

The Price of Nonconformance in Manufacturing is more than our pretax profit. *124*

We can't afford to have a $100 million leak in our boat, and more importantly we can't fail to manage the company so it will survive and grow. *126*

People can't have pride in a company that treats anyone harshly. *127*

Tough in this case doesn't mean beating up on people, of course. It refers to being able to stick to the necessary policies and actions no matter how enticing the reasons for easing up. *127*

The typical CEO takes office determined to reign rather than direct. *127*

Authority can be delegated, but only after it has been packaged. *127*

I have always been secretly afraid that someone was going to catch up with me one day.   *128*

But in the paperwork-computer world there are many more causes to choose from. We actually have a great deal more rework in Insurance than they do in Manufacturing.   *162*

It was beginning to become clear to me that these people did not attach the slightest significance to these ESO ratings.   *132*

The way we managed was destructive.   *132*

If everything is positioned correctly and we are working on the right things, then the company runs the way we want it. Otherwise, we just go from day to day, patching and fixing.   *134*

But the wellness I am talking about refers to the actions we take in order to avoid not being sick.   *135*

There are a lot of things that people can do when they think management is interested.   *135*

When we don't have to use up computer time debugging programs, we have what amounts to a 30 percent increase in capacity.   *135*

Our mission is to lay out the beginning of a strategy to make the company eternally successful.   *136*

At present we are not very people-oriented, and success is measured only by financial returns.   *136*

You want a whole new world, not just a new deal.   *136*

When an individual goes to a personal wellness center, the first thing that happens is the creation of a personal profile.   *137*

You really think this company can be restructured so that it meets the criteria for wellness?   *137*

We need to have a managerial purpose that gives us a permanent edge over the others.   *137*

We can't continue spending all that money doing things wrong on purpose.   *137*

People are learning a different and more effective way of dealing with a subject. *138*

"Growth that is profitable and steady" is the result of good strategic direction. *138*

"Customer needs are the priority" refers more to new products than anything else. *138*

"Change is planned and managed" is something we have begun to work on internally by developing Systems Integrity. *139*

People are hard to figure sometimes. Who knows what makes them proud? *139*

Every day we take is a day the company slips a bit more down the embankment. *139*

You think we couldn't create something that will last? *143*

People are really out for themselves. They don't think about the company as a whole. *144*

It will take a complete brain transplant to change this outfit. *144*

There is a solution to everything if we want to work at it. *144*

They do not get done routinely because prevention is not in keeping with the systems and priorities we have been raised to think are important. *145*

The key to anything like we are going to try is a clear identification for the individuals involved of what is in it for them. *146*

Consensus management was never one of the things I selected as the way to run a company. *146*

I have come to believe in the face of conventional wisdom that committees often make the best decisions. *146*

If you do harmful things to yourself, your life span gets shorter. *146*

They just cannot think about the corporation as a whole and forget what they do for a living. *147*

This was just one pothole along the road. It would have to be filled in and eliminated.   *147*

You mean describe a profile for a business in the same format as that for a person?   *149*

Good health is not something that just occurs, nor is it a gift from heaven. The managerial actions necessary to produce it are not automatically known to us. As far as I can see, running a body is a perfect analogy for running a business.   *149*

Taking the time to prevent is hard to justify in the mind of a busy person.   *150*

Providing original solutions to complex problems is a lot more interesting than not having the problem in the first place.   *150*

It is hard to recognize what didn't happen and the reason for it.   *150*

Actually it is more comfortable and a lot more fun to live this way than to slog around all the time.   *151*

There is nothing like putting on a sweat suit and watching other folks work out to make you feel like a real athlete.   *152*

The communicable diseases that used to reduce the population have been contained for the most part. So people live longer, but they don't necessarily have the active lives they could have.   *153*

Most of the stress we face is something we cause ourselves.   *153*

A lot of stress comes in over the phone and in the papers.   *153*

Nonsmokers have 30 percent fewer health care claims than smokers.   *153*

The all-time champion cholesterol container is liver.   *155*

It would be possible to bury an organization in all these

worthwhile things to the point that nothing else got done. *156*

The ESO characteristics represent good corporate health. *157*

We recognize that most of our problems are caused by management action, or lack of it. *157*

There are many advantages of predictability, and I think that is what being consistent brings about. *160*

Whenever management does anything successful, or solves a complex situation, it always seems to forget the whole thing and go on to something else. *160*

Let's make a rule that we can't use anything I can't explain in five minutes. *160*

What good is a department store without sales? *161*

When you decide to change a culture, you'd better be sure you know exactly what is getting changed. *161*

There can be no success, regardless of the soundness of the concept, if there is no understanding. *161*

People learn better when the instructor is someone who can affect their lives. *162*

One of the major problems we have is that people think the corporation does not care about their future. *163*

Sometimes management teams get so confident they doze off. *164*

We could learn a lot from the military basic training. *164*

It was not easy to found a company if you were irascible and untrustworthy. *169*

Companies have different products and markets, but they all have people. *169*

Many managements are sitting around contemplating rather than trying to do something about it. *170*

"Formalize success." *170*

The future has always been difficult to handle, but now it is really a challenge that requires a broad input.   *171*

It would be nice if there were just one specific set of actions a management group could take in order to produce success.   *173*

The investors figured something so well thought out can't be anything but successful.   *173*

To prevent the failure of a company, it is necessary to put things into perspective.   *174*

Companies, and industries, die because executives did not think of what is yet to come.   *174*

People working on the same thing can have a long conversation without ever using a proper word.   *174*

The heart and soul of a corporation do not lie in its products. Rather it rests in the process that produces the output of the organization.   *175*

You have noticed that many nations never seem to progress.   *175*

The problem is in the process, and that working at the wrong end of it creates nothing of lasting worth.   *176*

Just providing low-level jobs is not much more than a welfare program that makes everyone feel less guilty about it all.   *176*

The problem is in the process.   *176*

Business organizations usually do not recognize that the product is the result of the culture of the organization, not the other way around.   *176*

Athletic teams concentrate on attitude, pride, and basics.   *176*

Higher education organizations create an environment in which learning is a desirable venture.   *176*

Cultures can be created once a basic set of principles has been defined and understood.   *176*

You can see that insurance had an annual PONC rate of $52

million, or $1 million a week. That rate has dropped by one-third in the first year. *178*

So far we are talking about an annual reduction of $47 million, all due to reeducating management and employees to understand quality in the same way. *178*

Quality is a choice management can make. *178*

Growing is something a company has to do if it is to be around forever. *178*

Growth is part of wellness. *178*

The real basis for growth often comes from knowing how to use better what is already around. *179*

Mental development in the individual is what brings success and recognition. *179*

Wellness is no accident. *179*

New products and services appear as needed and customer desire is met even before customers are aware that it is important to them. *179*

Development is done deliberately and innovatively. *179*

Communication, example, and participation are the three legs of the platform for pride. *179*

Why some companies choose to be rude and insensitive to their employees is something I have never understood. *179*

Senior management bears a large part of the responsibility in creating an environment in which pride is encouraged to blossom. *180*

Prevention pays off and pays its own way. *180*

Companies are dictatorships regardless of all the talk about consensus and participative management. *181*

The employees of the company do not believe that they, as individuals, are integral components of the organization. *184*

Information systems are just not up to what we need. *184*

Many people do not need much success to take something off the problem list.   *185*   .

The quality improvement effort is not embedded into the company, its systems, its suppliers, its customers, and its people.   *186*

The internal information system program is too narrow to permit true business communications throughout the company.   *186*

The performance evaluation program and the personnel compensation system do not reward merit or encourage innovation.   *186*

Senior management is not reasonably available to participate on a regular basis and is not actively listening.   *186*

Employees, while loyal to the company, do not feel personal ownership to the point necessary for a massive improvement effort.   *187*

We do not have a proven way of knowing what customers are thinking about or needing.   *187*

The margins are beginning to become smaller each year, and the cash flow is a little less, proportionally, than it was. This has tended to delay projects and reduce options.   *187*

The base of the company is too narrow, having two divisions, in two businesses that do not feed each other.   *187*

Top managers have always been traditionally dependent on lower managers to keep them informed and to provide specific knowledge about specific things.   *188*

Top managers are forever setting up systems and programs to make everything run more efficiently, but they don't use them personally, and they don't participate with others that do use them.   *188*

But the fact of real life is that in most companies the chairperson and president make it all up as they go along.   *188*

Programs work only if they reflect accurately the behavior and thought processes of the head shed.   *190*

It isn't the system or the law; it is the local environment. You can't fool people on these things.   *190*

They are all designed to make things convenient for the evaluator, not to help the individual.   *191*

Performance reviews probably do more to make employees antagonistic to their company than any other single item.   *191*

If their summary data were on your screen regularly, they would know it and so would you.   *191*

But there is an answer, and it revolves around the respect they think the company has or doesn't have for them.   *192*

In the same agency you can find herds of people who feel deeply respected and herds of people in open revolt.   *192*

Customer research is a never-ending operation.   *192*

The management approaches and cultures that have become normal over the years just may not be enough to guarantee success.   *196*

We have traded Bob Cratchet's quill pen for a word processor, but the procedure is still the same.   *196*

The real problem is in what action we actually take to learn how to prevent such situations from ever happening at all.   *197*

It is quite clear that it is a very rare instance when a problem was so well solved and prevented that it disappeared forever.   *197*

We need to learn how to spend our time and effort working on the future instead of continually rearranging the past.   *197*

If we take care not to get sick, then we don't need to take the measures necessary to become well again.   *197*

We are learning to prevent problems rather than develop unique actions to solve them.   *197*

All of us have to learn how to prevent problems and at the

same time grow the next generation of executives, managers, knowledge workers, and skilled employees.   *197*

We have...to understand how to help the customers in ways they haven't even thought about yet.   *198*

We have...to grow in a manner that is continually profitable and prepares us for the future.   *198*

I think we should look at our incentive compensation plan and realize that people just think of it as another way of getting their pay in a slow fashion.   *198*

We need to learn how to manage our customer relations so that we don't have ups and downs that require layoffs.   *198*

There is a lot to be said for consistent employment, and it is a lot less expensive to handle.   *198*

Creating an environment that lets people feel like part of a family establishes a concern for the company's health and welfare that does not exist today.   *199*

It is the difference between participating in the excitement of learning with others or taking lonely TV courses.   *199*

A college provides a person with an identity; solo courses just provide information.   *199*

It is the difference between doing things on purpose and reacting to what is happening.   *199*

I think we can innovate and execute continually without lurching from semidisaster to real disaster.   *199*

Managerial skills and techniques won't save us.   *199*

It is very easy to become complacent and slip away from communicating.   *200*

The consumer product companies, which have hundreds of different products, put someone in charge of each one.   *200*

It will take forever, but then that is how long we have.   *200*

Field people would not tell everything they knew because

they didn't want to be criticized, and because they thought the people back here wouldn't do anything anyway.   *204*

Not everyone recognizes change when he or she sees it.   *204*

It is very hard to have outside executives teach inside executives.   *204*

It wasn't until we began to combine literal ownership with credible performance appraisal that things began to change.   *205*

It is hard to believe how well-intentioned people can mistreat their associates.   *206*

Take care of the employees and the customers; the rest will take care of itself.   *214*

The best way to understand something is to become involved in its development and implementation.   *217*

Quality has to be caused, not controlled.   *217*

The good news was that many companies were interested in obtaining the services offered; the bad news was that all this was very expensive and time-consuming to start up and establish.   *218*

Index

About the Author

Philip B. Crosby is CEO of Philip Crosby Associates, Inc., the international quality-management consulting firm he founded in 1979 in Winter Park, Florida. Philip Crosby Associates is now a public company. Crosby was Corporate Vice President of ITT for 14 years. He is the author of *Quality Is Free* (1979); *Quality Without Tears* (1984); *The Art of Getting Your Own Sweet Way* (1972 and 1981); and *Running Things* (1986)—all McGraw-Hill titles.